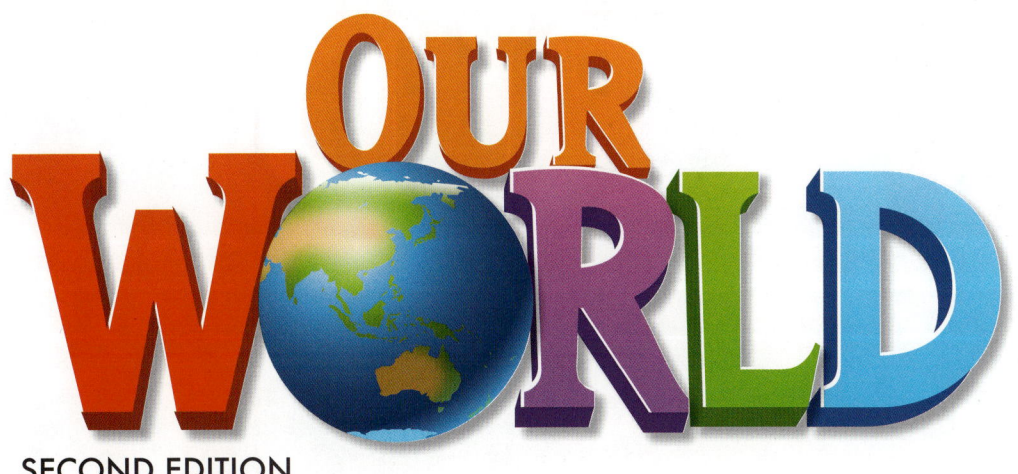

Our World

SECOND EDITION

Series Editors
Joan Kang Shin and
JoAnn (Jodi) Crandall

Student's Book Author
Rob Sved

Australia • Brazil • Mexico • Singapore • United Kingdom • United States

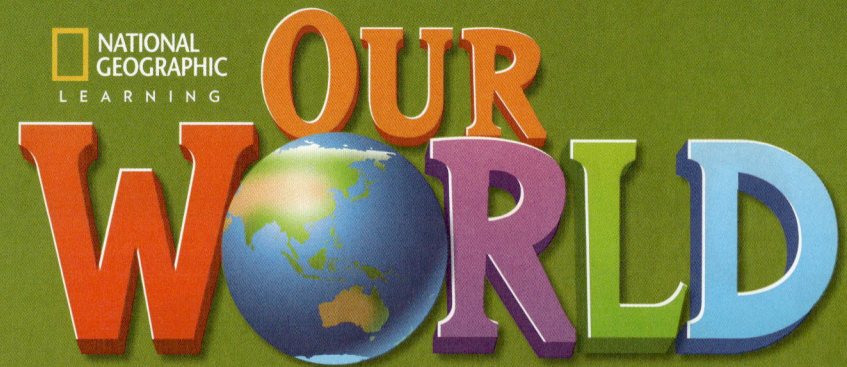

TR: 10.1

This is our world.
Everybody's got a song to sing.
Each boy and girl.
This is our world!
I say "our." You say "world."
Our!
World!
Our!
World!
I say "boy." You say "girl."
Boy!
Girl!
Boy!
Girl!
I say, "Everybody move!"
I say, "Everybody stop!"
Everybody, stop!
This is our world.
Everybody's got a song to sing.
Each boy and girl.
This is our world!

SECOND EDITION

Student's Book
Unit 5 Animal Habitats...4
Unit 6 What's for Dinner?..20
Unit 7 Feeling Fit...36
Unit 8 Let's Celebrate!..52
Unit 9 My Weekend...68
Units 4-6 Extended Reading The Gingerbread Man.........84
Units 7-9 Extended Reading The Paralympics................86

Workbook
Unit 5 Animal Habitats..88
Unit 6 What's for Dinner?..100
Unit 7 Feeling Fit...112
Unit 8 Let's Celebrate!..124
Unit 9 My Weekend..136
Activities and Games..148

Student's Book
Cutouts...153
Stickers

Animal Habitats

In this unit, I will . . .
- name animal habitats.
- say what animals look like.
- talk about animal homes.

Look and circle.

1. This is a _____.
    a. gorilla   b. hippo   c. panda

2. He's holding a _____.
    a. leaf   b. fruit   c. toy

Silverback gorilla, Democratic Republic of the Congo

VOCABULARY 1

1 Listen and read. TR: 5.1

2 Listen and say. TR: 5.2

We all need a place to live. We live in houses or apartments in our neighborhood. Animals and plants have a place to live, too. This place is called their habitat.

wetlands

grasslands

a forest

a rain forest

a desert

Tenere Desert, Niger

6 Unit 5

 ice

 snow

 mud

 a web

 a hive

 a nest

 underground

 an island

 a cave

3 **Work with a partner.** Ask and answer.

Where do camels live?

They live in the desert.

SONG

1 **Listen.** Read and sing. TR: 5.3

Why? Because!

Why does a giraffe have a long, long neck?
Why?
Why?
Because it eats leaves at the tops of the trees.

I want to know why.
I want to know why.
Why?
Because I want to know why!

Why does a frog have strong legs?
Why?
Why?
Because it hops, swims, and jumps.

CHORUS

Animals are amazing.
They do so many things.
And I have just one thing to say.
Why?

Why does a polar bear have white fur?
Why?
Why?
Because it lives in ice and snow.

CHORUS

2 **Act out and describe an animal.**
Work with a group. Your group guesses the animal. Take turns.

Wallace's flying frog,
Kuala Lumpur, Malaysia

GRAMMAR 1

Why... ? Because ... TR: 5.4

Why does a giraffe have a long neck? **Because** it eats leaves at the top of trees.
Why don't you like penguins? **Because** they look silly, and they can't fly!

1 Match.

1. Why do jaguars have spots?

a. Because they eat meat.

2. Why does a polar bear cover its black nose?

b. Because they need to hide in the trees.

3. Why do crocodiles have sharp teeth?

c. Because it can't fly, and it needs to run fast.

4. Why does an owl have big eyes?

d. Because it wants to hide in the snow.

5. Why does an ostrich have long legs?

e. Because it needs to see at night.

2 **Read the answers.** Then write a question with *why* for each answer.

1. _____

   Because they catch insects in them.

2. _____

   Because they lay their eggs and raise their babies in them.

3. _____

   Because they need a place to keep their honey.

4. _____

   Because we need a place to stay warm and safe.

3 **Ask and answer.** Talk about these animals. Work with a partner.

elephant   monkey   parrot   penguin   spider

Why do you like parrots?

Because they're colorful and smart!

11

VOCABULARY 2

1 Listen and say. Write the animals in the correct groups. TR: 5.5

| butterfly | cat | duck | goat | kangaroo |
| monkey | ~~parrot~~ | penguin | polar bear | rabbit |

pouch	fur	wings	horns
		parrot	

2 Guess and stick. Work with a partner.

— This animal is big and white. It lives in the snow. It has sharp claws.
— It's a polar bear!

1   2   3   4   5

GRAMMAR 2

Infinitive of purpose TR: 5.6
Giraffes use their long tongues **to clean** their ears.
Goats use their horns **to fight.**

1 **Read and match.** Then say in pairs.

1. Zebras use their black and white fur
2. Cats use their tongues
3. Kangaroos use their pouches
4. Elephants use their long trunks
5. Tigers use their sharp teeth
6. Penguins use their wings

a. to carry their babies.
b. to eat meat.
c. to clean their fur.
d. to swim in the ocean.
e. to shower.
f. to hide in the grasslands.

2 **Play a game.** Cut out the cubes in the back of the book. Work with a partner. Make sentences.

Dogs use their trunks to drink water.

That's not true! Elephants use their trunks to drink water! Dogs don't have trunks!

READING

1 Listen and read. TR: 5.7

Amazing Rain Forests

Rain forests are warm, wet forests. They are in countries near the equator—in Central America, South America, Africa, Southeast Asia, and Australia. Rain forests are important. They're homes for millions of animals and plants. The plants in rain forests make much of the oxygen that people in the world need to live.

A RAIN FOREST HAS FOUR PARTS:

Emergent
In this part, you can see the tops of very tall trees. They are sometimes 60 m (200 ft.) tall! Many different birds, butterflies, and other insects live here.

Canopy
In this part of the forest, the trees have many leaves. Birds, spiders, tree frogs, monkeys, and snakes live here.

Understory
In this part of the forest, it is dark, wet, and cool. There aren't many plants. Why? Because plants need light to live. Snakes and lizards live here. Jaguars like to live in this part, too!

Forest floor
In this part, there are many insects and spiders. Some spiders are as big as plates! There are many large animals. And people live here, too!

Howler monkeys are very, very loud. You can hear them from 5 km (3 mi.) away.

2 **Read.** Circle the correct words.

1. Rain forests are in countries **far from / near** the equator.

2. Plants make a lot of **oxygen / water.**

3. Plants need **light / oxygen** to live.

4. Many **leopards / birds** live in the top part of the rain forest.

5. Many large animals live on the **forest floor / tops of trees.**

3 **Complete the chart.** Use these words. You can use some words more than once.

birds   dark   large animals   monkeys   snakes   spiders   sunny

4 **Talk about the different parts of the rain forest.**
Work with a partner.

There are gorillas in this part.

15

WRITING

1 **Read about Mounira's animal.** Underline words that tell you what the animal looks like. Write the name of the animal.

My name is Mounira. I live by the Nile River. This animal lives here. What is it? Can you guess?

It lives in the river. It's brown and it has black spots on its back. It has four short legs and a long tail. It has big eyes on top of its head, and it uses them to see above the water. It has a strong mouth and sharp teeth! It can walk and it can swim.

It is scary, but I like it!

Yes! It's a _____.

2 **Write about an animal you like.**

3 **Share your writing.** Work in a small group. Listen and fill in the chart.

Name	Animal	Where it lives	What it looks like

VALUES

Help protect animal habitats.

Think. Pair. Share.

- Why is it important to protect animal habitats?
- How can you help protect animal habitats?

Maasai Mara National Reserve, Kenya

PROJECT

Make a mobile of an animal habitat. Choose a habitat and animals.

Choose an animal and draw it.

Research your animal's habitat. What other animals and plants live there?

Draw these animals and plants.

Hang the pictures on your mobile.

Unit 6
What's for Dinner?

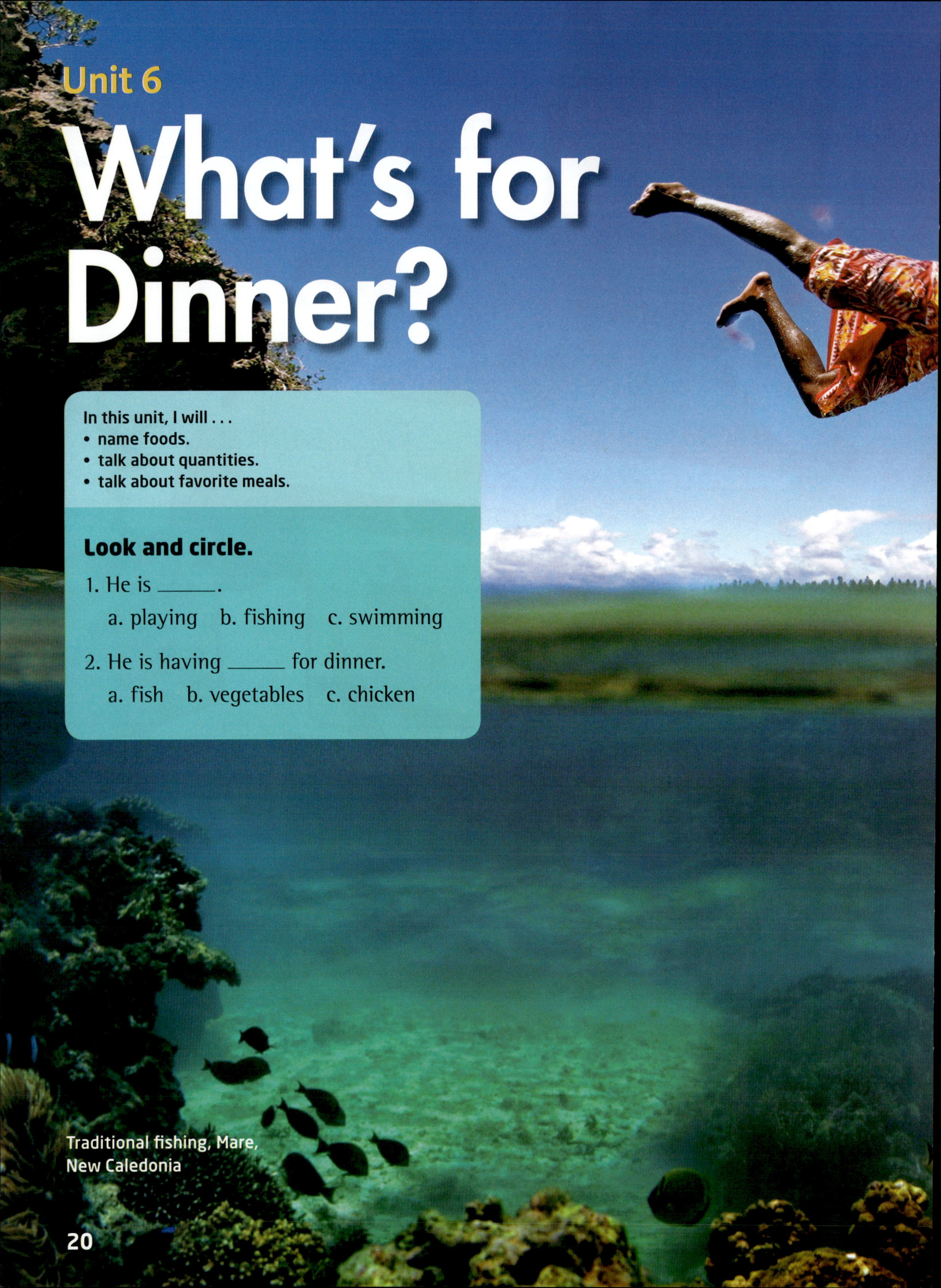

In this unit, I will . . .
- name foods.
- talk about quantities.
- talk about favorite meals.

Look and circle.

1. He is _____.
   a. playing   b. fishing   c. swimming

2. He is having _____ for dinner.
   a. fish   b. vegetables   c. chicken

Traditional fishing, Mare, New Caledonia

VOCABULARY 1

1 Listen and read. TR: 6.1

2 Listen and say. TR: 6.2

We all love food. We can find food in stores or at the market. What's your favorite food? Let's go shopping!

a bottle of oil

a bag of rice

a loaf of bread

a jar of olives

CORN
FLAKES

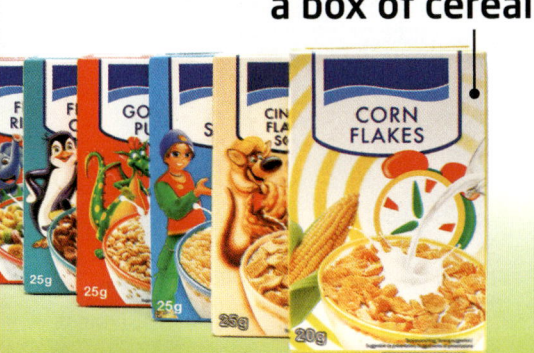

a box of cereal

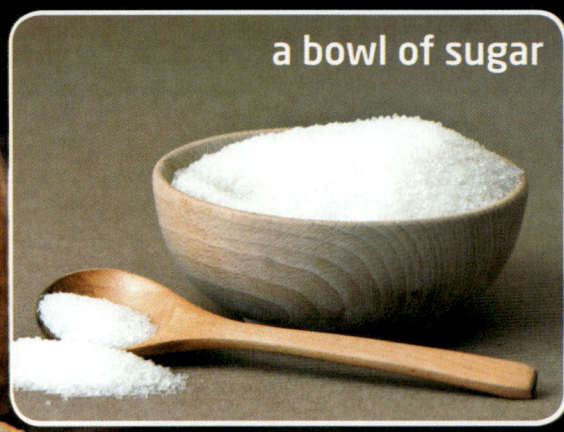

a bowl of sugar

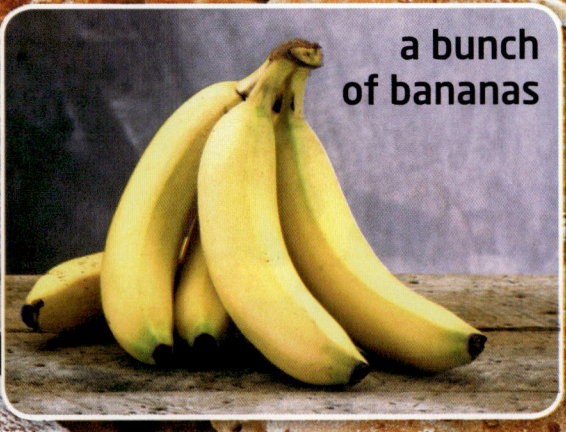

a bunch of bananas

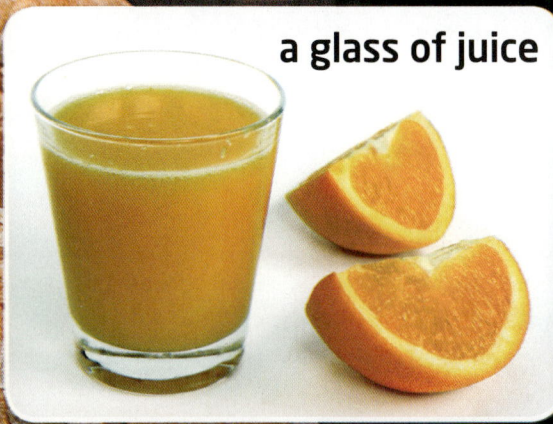

a glass of juice

FRESH
COLA
DRINK

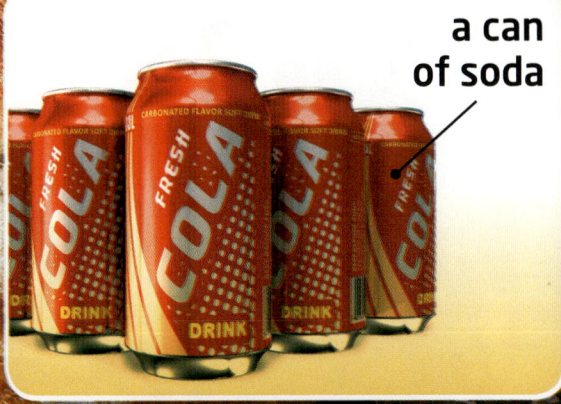

a can of soda

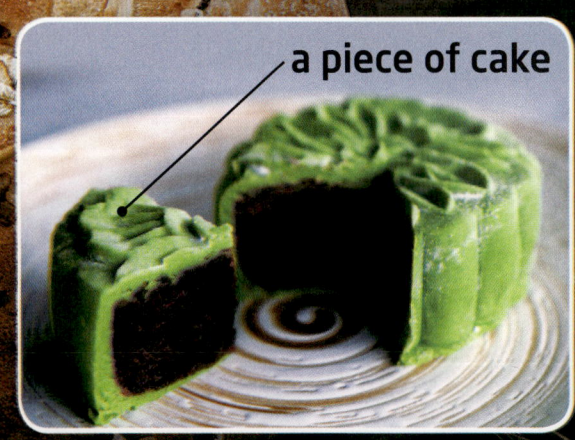

a piece of cake

3 **Say what you see.** Work with a partner. Add to the sentence each time.

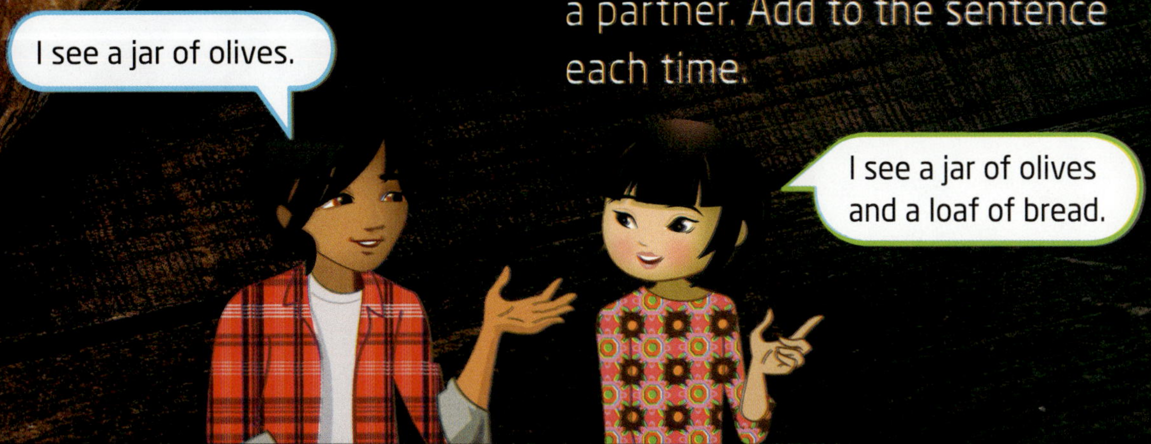
I see a jar of olives.
I see a jar of olives and a loaf of bread.

SONG

1 **Listen.** Read and sing. TR: 6.3

Let's Go Shopping!

**Let's go shopping. Let's go shopping,
let's go shopping today.
Let's go shopping to buy some food,
then go home to put it away.**

A jar of jelly is no fun,
if there isn't any bread to spread it on.
A bowl of rice is very nice,
but it tastes better with some spice.

CHORUS

Let's buy some pasta at the shop,
and some sauce to put on top.
Let's buy a cake. Cake's a treat.
I like cake because it's sweet!

A bowl of pasta, a jar of spice,
a glass of juice, and cake are nice!
Let's go now. Let's buy some food.
Let's go shopping, just me and you!

CHORUS

2 **Sing.** Find and point. Work with a partner.

25

GRAMMAR 1

some and **any** TR: 6.4

Are there **any** oranges?   Yes, there are **some** in the fruit bowl.
Are there **any** bananas?   No, there aren't **any**.
Is there **any** milk?   Yes, there is **some** in the fridge.
Is there **any** bread?   No, there isn't **any**.

1 **Read.** Look and write answers.

1. Are there any tomatoes? *Yes, there is one on the table.*

2. Is there any rice? _____

3. Are there any olives? _____

4. Are there any grapes? _____

5. Is there any sugar? _____

6. Are there any bananas _____

26 Unit 6

2 **Ask and answer.** Look at the food in the picture. Work with a partner. Take turns.

Is there any yogurt?

No, there isn't any.

VOCABULARY 2

1 **Listen and say.** Read and write. TR: 6.5

money

put away

a price

compare

buy

1. Which drink is better for you? Let's _____ them.
   a. buy   b. compare   c. eat

2. Can you help me _____ the food in the fridge, please?
   a. compare   b. put away   c. buy

3. The _____ of that loaf of bread is ninety cents.
   a. price   b. money   c. buy

4. Let's _____ some milk. We don't have any.
   a. compare   b. put away   c. buy

2 **Listen and stick.** Work with a partner. TR: 6.6

| 1 | 2 | 3 | 4 | 5 |

28 Unit 6

GRAMMAR 2

a few and a little TR: 6.7

Are there any cookies?　　　　　　　Yes, there are **a few**.
Is there any orange juice?　　　　　　Yes, there is **a little**.

1　Read and write.

1. Is there any ice cream? Yes, there _____.

2. Are there any peppers? Yes, there _____.

3. Is there any rice? Yes, there _____.

4. Are there any potatoes? Yes, there _____.

2　Play a game. Cut out the board game and the cards in the back of the book. Put the cards on the board. Play with a partner.

B1. Is there any soda?

No, there isn't any soda.
A1. Are there any eggs?

Yes, there are a few. Here you are.

READING

1 Listen and read. TR: 6.8

What's for lunch

France

Millions of children around the world eat lunch at school. Some bring their lunch from home. Others eat food that the school makes for them. Schools in different countries make different kinds of lunches.

In France, children eat together in a cafeteria. They have a big lunch because they don't eat snacks in the morning. Sometimes they eat fish or sausages, with vegetables or salad. Then they may have fruit or a piece of cake.

Japan

In Japan, children usually eat their lunch in the classroom. They eat soup, rice or noodles, fish and vegetables. They drink milk, too. After lunch, all the children work together to clean the classroom.

In Brazil, children may eat rice and beans, salad, and cooked vegetables or meat for lunch. And sometimes they eat fruit, as well.

Brazil

In Russia, children eat vegetable soup and fish or meat with bread. One delicious soup, called borscht, is made with dark red vegetables called beets.

Russia

30 Unit 6

2 Read. Check T for *True* and F for *False*.

1. In France, children eat lunch outside.   T F
2. In France, children sometimes eat fruit with lunch.   T F
3. In Japan, children help clean the classroom together after lunch.   T F
4. In Russia, children sometimes eat soup for lunch.   T F
5. In Brazil, many children eat rice and beans.   T F

3 Read. Complete the chart.

Country	Where do they eat?	What they sometimes eat
France		
Russia		
Japan		
Brazil		

4 Talk about what the people eat. What do you eat? Work with a partner.

Every day half the people in the world eat rice.

I have cereal for breakfast.

I do, too!

WRITING

1 Read. In a paragraph, the first sentence is called the *topic sentence*. It tells the main idea. The other sentences are called the *body* of the paragraph. They give more information about that idea.

My Favorite Meal

I love all kinds of food, but I have one favorite meal. First, I have a small bowl of chicken soup. Then I have a burger. Burgers are delicious! I love burgers! I like them with cheese, lettuce, and tomatoes. Then I have strawberries with vanilla ice cream and chocolate sauce. Yum! And sometimes I have a big glass of cold milk with everything! Yum!

2 Write. Write about your favorite meal. Then check your writing. Circle *yes* or *no*.

Does your first sentence tell what the paragraph is about?   **Yes   No**

Do the other sentences give more information about it?   **Yes   No**

3 Share your writing. Work in a small group. Listen and fill the chart.

Name	Favorite meal

VALUES

Eat good food.

Think about what you eat.

Rothschild's giraffes, Woburn Safari Park, England

Think. Pair. Share.

- Why is it important to eat good food?
- Why should you read the labels on boxes and cans?

PROJECT

Organize a Taste Test Day. Taste food together. Describe each food. How does it taste?

Bring in different kinds of food.

Work with a partner. Put on a blindfold and taste the food.

Interview your partner. Write down descriptions.

Take turns writing and tasting!

Unit 7
Feeling Fit

In this unit, I will . . .
- name parts of the body.
- talk about the past.
- talk about good and bad habits.

Check T for *True* and F for *False*.

1. He is climbing.　　　　　　　T　F
2. He is using his hands and feet.　　T　F
3. He is wearing a blue shirt.　　T　F

Climbing the tsingy in Madagascar. *Tsingy* means "Where you cannot walk barefoot."

VOCABULARY 1

1 Listen and read. TR: 7.1

2 Listen and say. TR: 7.2

It's important to take care of your body. Exercise and good food help keep you fit and healthy.

a muscle

fingers

a chest

a stomach

Khmer classical dance, Siem Reap, Cambodia

a knee

a bone

38 Unit 7

a shoulder

an elbow

a back

toes

stretch

bend

3 **Say, listen, and do.**
Work with a partner.

Stretch your arms!

OK. My turn.

39

SONG

1 **Listen.** Read and sing. TR: 7.3

Let's Move

We like to feel fit.
We like to have fun.
We like to play hard.
Let's move now, everyone!

CHORUS
We want to feel healthy.
We want to feel fit.
Come on, everybody.
Stand! Don't sit!

What did you do to be fit today?
What did you do to be strong?
What did you do to be fit today?
What did you do?

Did you move your legs? Yes, I did!
Did you stretch your back? I did that a lot!
Did you get enough sleep? Yes, I did!
Did you eat a healthy snack? Oops, I forgot!

Don't worry. Tomorrow is another day.
You can try again. It's OK!

We like to feel fit.
We like to have fun.
We like to play hard.
Let's jump now, everyone!

CHORUS

Limbo skating, New Delhi, India

What did you do to be fit today?
What did you do to be strong?
What did you do to be fit today?
What did you do?

Did you stretch your muscles? Yes, I did!
Did you touch your toes? I did that a lot!
Did you bend your knees? Yes, I did!
Did you wiggle your nose? No. I forgot!

Don't worry. Tomorrow is another day.
You can try again. It's OK!

We like to feel fit.
We like to have fun.
We like to play hard.
Let's dance now, everyone!

CHORUS

2 **Act out an activity.**
Work with a group. Take turns.

41

GRAMMAR 1

Simple past: Yes / No questions and short answers TR: 7.4

Did you **wash** your hands?   Yes, I **did**.
Did you **brush** your teeth?   No, I **didn't**.
Did he **take** a shower?   Yes, he **did**.

1 **Read and look.** Write answers.

1. Did he take a shower yesterday? _No, he didn't._

2. Did she brush her teeth? _____

3. Did she eat fruit? _____

4. Did he go for a walk? _____

5. Did he ride his bike? _____

6. Did she make her bed? _____

42 Unit 7

2 **Write.** What about you? Complete the questions and answers.

1. _Did you ride_ your bike yesterday? _No, I didn't._
2. _____ your teeth yesterday? _____
3. _____ a snack yesterday? _____
4. _____ make your bed today? _____
5. _____ soccer yesterday? _____
6. _____ your hands yesterday? _____
7. _____ TV yesterday? _____
8. _____ your homework yesterday? _____

3 **Ask and answer questions.** Use these words. Work in a group.

| do your homework | eat salad | go for a walk |
| make your bed | play basketball | swim |

Did you go for a walk yesterday?

Yes, I did.

VOCABULARY 2

1 Listen and say. Read and write. TR: 7.5

eat junk food

eat vegetables

get exercise

get rest

eat fruit

1. I _____ every day. I like apples, mangoes, and grapes!

2. I _____ every day. I play soccer and go swimming.

3. I _____ every day. I love carrots, beans, and potatoes.

4. I _____ every day. I relax after exercise, and I sleep at night!

5. I _____ sometimes. I like to eat potato chips and drink soda!

2 Stick in order (1 = most important). Work with a partner. Talk about what you think is important.

My number one is exercise. It's very important to get exercise.

My number one is fruit. I think it's important to eat fruit.

1   2   3   4   5

44 Unit 7

GRAMMAR 2

too and enough TR: 7.6

I don't watch **too much** TV. I think I get **enough** exercise.
I drink **enough** water. I don't eat **too much** junk food.

1 **Read and make true sentences about you.**
Underline the words and complete the sentences.

| enough | too many | too much |

1. I **drink / don't drink** _____ soda.

2. I **get / don't get** _____ exercise.

3. I **drink / don't drink** _____ water.

4. I **eat / don't eat** _____ chips.

5. I **watch / don't watch** _____ TV.

6. I **get / don't get** _____ sleep.

2 **Play a game.** Cut out the cards in the back of the book. Choose a card and flip a coin. Play with a partner.

Heads = good for you    **Tails =** bad for you

Tails. I watch too much TV. No points for me! Your turn.

Heads. I get enough sleep. One point for me!

45

READING

1 Listen and read. TR: 7.7

Take Care of Your BRAIN!

We all know that it's important to exercise, but we don't always want to do it. Some people think that exercising every day is too hard, or that it takes too long. They think they don't have time to exercise every day.

Well, here's some good news! If you exercise for only ten minutes a day, your body *and* your brain will feel better! In fact, some scientists believe that ten minutes of exercise every day can make you think faster and smarter!

Exercise isn't the only thing that's good for your brain. Scientists believe that spending time outside is also great for your brain and your body. They know that your brain relaxes when you're outdoors in a natural place like a forest. Some scientists think people should take a "forest bath," or spend time in an outdoor place, whenever they can.

Even laughing is good for your brain! When you laugh, especially if you laugh out loud, your brain gets more blood than when you're sad! Your whole body can feel better for up to 45 minutes after a good laugh!

Think about it. Are you taking good care of your brain? Do you get enough exercise? Do you spend enough time outdoors? Do you laugh enough?

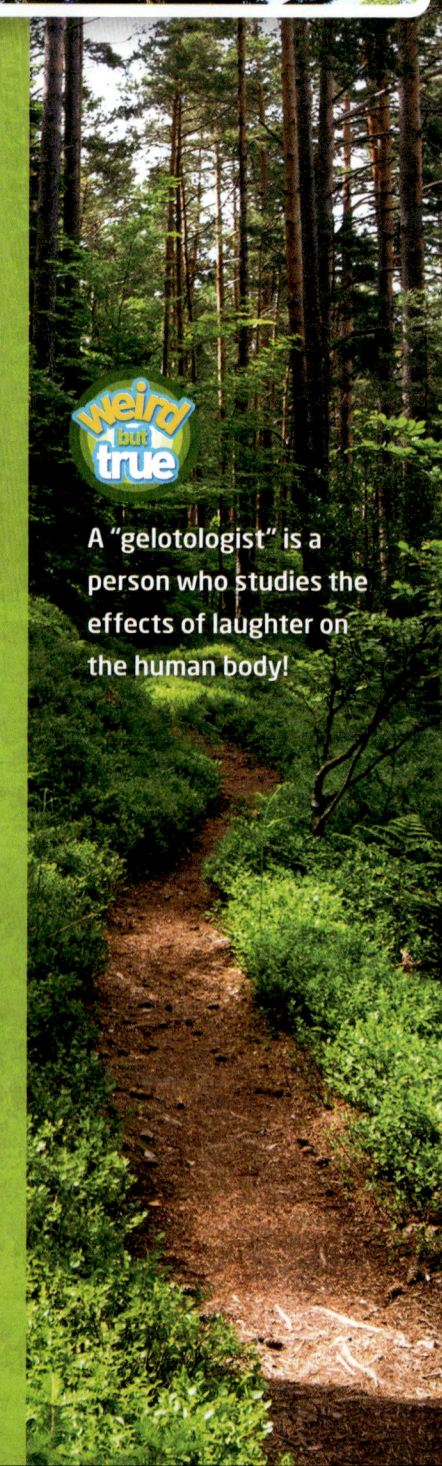

Weird but true

A "gelotologist" is a person who studies the effects of laughter on the human body!

2 **Read and underline.**

1. Exercise is **good / bad** for your body and brain.

2. If you exercise for ten **hours / minutes** a day, your brain will feel better.

3. You have to be **outdoors / indoors** to take a forest bath.

4. Your body can feel better for 45 minutes after you **laugh / exercise** out loud.

5. It's important to **watch TV / exercise** every day.

3 **Write.** Why is exercise good for...

your body?	your brain?

4 **Ask and answer.** Work with a partner. Do you like to exercise? What do you like to do?

I like to exercise!

Me, too! I like to jump rope and play outdoors.

WRITING

1 Read. Read about Daniel's favorite way to keep fit. He uses *because* to explain why he likes swimming.

Swim to Keep Fit!

Swimming is my favorite way to keep fit. It's great exercise and a lot of fun, too! I like it because you move all of your body. You use your arms, your shoulders, your legs—and all your muscles.

Another reason I like it is because you can swim inside or outside. In winter I go to the swimming pool. In summer I sometimes swim in the sea. I like that because it feels different. I like to swim in races, too. But my favorite thing is to splash water and have fun with my friends!

2 Write. Do you keep fit? What exercise or sport do you like? Why?

3 Share your writing. Work in a small group. Listen and fill the chart.

Name	Activity	Why

48 Unit 7

VALUE

Keep fit.

Take care of your body.
Exercise.

Think. Pair. Share.

Do you exercise?
What do you like to do?

Central Park, New York City, USA

PROJECT

Make a poster. Work in a group. Make a *Good Habits* poster.

1. Make four sections on your paper.

2. Write the headings: *Keep fit, Stay clean, Eat good food, Keep safe.*

3. Write sentences, and draw or cut out pictures.

4. Sign your name.

Now I can . . .

○ name parts of the body.
○ talk about the past.
○ talk about good and bad habits.

We think it's important to sleep eight hours every night.

Good Habits

Keep fit
- Sleep eight hours every night.
- Do some exercise every day.

Stay Clean
- Wash your hands before meals.
- Brush your teeth every morning and night.

Eat good food
- Eat lots of fruit and vegetables.
- Have healthy snacks.

Keep safe
- On your bike, wear clothes to protect you.
- Be careful when you walk outside.

Mi Young   Jae Sun

Unit 8

Let's Celebrate

The Carnival of Oruro, Oruro, Bolivia

In this unit, I will . . .
- talk about celebrations and festivals.
- tell what happened in the past.
- talk about cultural traditions.

Look and check.

1. These people are
   - ⭕ celebrating.
   - ⭕ resting.

2. They are wearing colorful
   - ⭕ costumes.
   - ⭕ bathing suits.

People all over the world have special celebrations. They take time to remember the past, meet family and friends, eat food, and have fun!

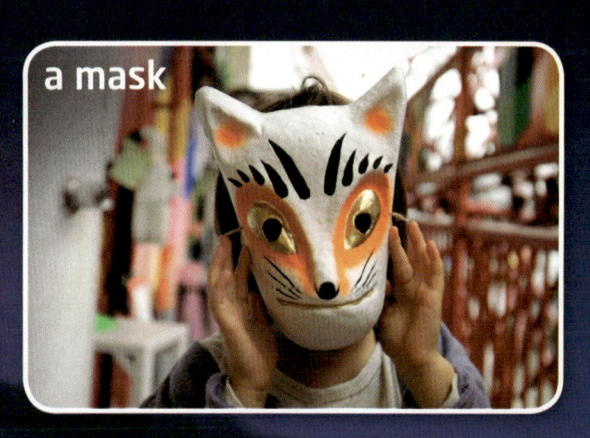

a costume

a feast

a mask

a lantern

a party

fireworks

54 Unit 8

celebrate

remember

dance

dress up

decorations

a parade

3 **Work with a partner.** Ask and answer.

Do you like to dress up?

Yes, I do. I have many costumes.

SONG

1 **Listen.** Read and sing. TR: 8.3

Celebrate!

We went to a carnival.
Everyone was there!
We dressed up, sang some songs,
and watched a parade.

But best of all,
we danced to music,
wonderful music.
We danced to music
all day long.

CHORUS
We danced to music,
wonderful music.
We danced to music
all day long.

Did you like the food?
Yes, I liked the food.
Did you dress up?
Yes, I went as a frog.

CHORUS

Did you like the costumes?
Yes, I liked the costumes.
Did you see any masks?
Yes, we saw some masks.

CHORUS

Rio de Janeiro, Brazil

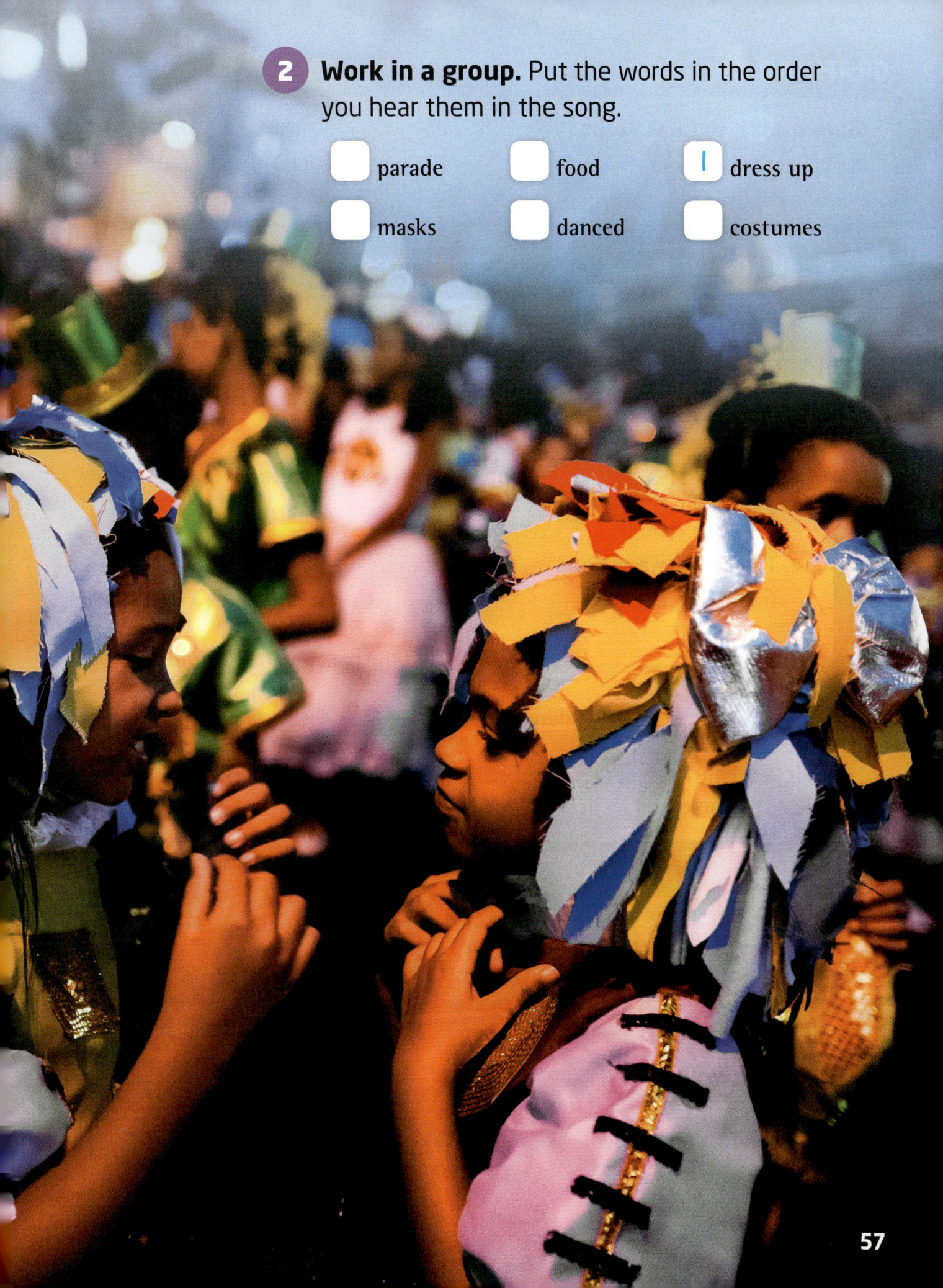

2 **Work in a group.** Put the words in the order you hear them in the song.

☐ parade ☐ food ☐ 1 dress up
☐ masks ☐ danced ☐ costumes

57

GRAMMAR 1

Simple past: regular verbs TR: 8.4

Did you **watch** the parade?
Did you **like** the music?

Yes, we **watched** the parade.
Yes, we **liked** it a lot!

1 **Read and write.** Complete the sentences. Use these words.

| dress up | like | listen | play | watch |

Yesterday . . .

1. I _____ in my favorite costume. I was a superhero!

2. The parade was great. We _____ to music from many countries.

3. I _____ the food and the dancing. It was fun!

4. After dinner all the children _____ games.

5. At night we _____ the fireworks. They were incredible!

58 Unit 8

2 **Write true sentences.** Think of a celebration.
Use these words.

| celebrate | dance | like | listen | play | watch |

1. _____
2. _____
3. _____
4. _____
5. _____
6. _____

3 **Ask questions about your celebrations.**
Work with a partner.

Did you play games at the party?

Yes, we played games. It was fun.

VOCABULARY 2

1 **Listen and say.**
Read and write. TR: 8.5

a birthday cake

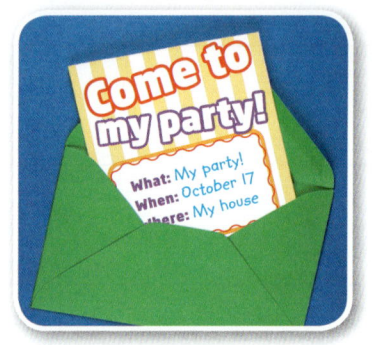

candles

a present

an invitation

balloons

1. You write this on paper. You give it to your friends. _____

2. It tastes sweet. It usually has candles on top. _____

3. They are usually round. They have air inside. _____

4. They are long and thin. You put them on a birthday cake. _____

5. You use colorful paper to wrap it. You give it to people on

   their birthdays. _____

2 **Listen and stick.** TR: 8.6

| 1 | 2 | 3 | 4 | 5 |

60 Unit 8

GRAMMAR 2

Simple past: irregular verbs TR: 8.7

Did you **go** to the parade? Yes, I **went** to the parade.
Did you **see** the fireworks? Yes, I **saw** the fireworks.
Did you **eat** cake at the party? Yes, I **ate** a piece of cake.

1 **Match.** These verbs change when you talk about the past. Draw lines. Work with a partner.

sing	wrote
drink	gave
wear	had
have	took
write	sang
give	drank
take	wore

2 **Play a game.** Cut out the cards in the back of the book. Play with a partner. Match and say sentences.

See. Saw. I saw lots of lanterns. Your turn.

No match for me. Your turn again.

61

READING

1 Listen and read. TR: 8.8

November Celebrations

The Day of the Dead is a big festival in Mexico. People celebrate it on the first day of November. They remember and celebrate the dead people in their families. They sometimes decorate the cemeteries with skeletons in special costumes. Families take a big feast to the cemetery, and they light candles and play music. People give candy and chocolate in the shape of skulls. For Mexicans, skulls and skeletons are not scary, and the festival is not sad. The Day of the Dead is a time for fun and happy celebrations.

In Thailand, the festival of Yi Peng usually happens in November, too. On the first day, there is a parade and people wear beautiful costumes. People make lanterns out of rice paper. They light small candles inside them. On the night of the festival, thousands of bright lanterns go up into the sky. People believe that the lanterns are taking away the bad things in their lives. People also decorate their homes and gardens with paper lanterns. And on the last day, there are fireworks.

Day of the Dead

Festival of Yi Peng

Weird but true

In 2002 a candy company made chocolate fireworks! 60 kg (132 lb.) of chocolate went up into the sky!

2 Read. Check **T** for *True* and **F** for *False*.

1. The Day of the Dead is a sad festival in Mexico.   (T) (F)

2. On the Day of the Dead, families eat food at the cemeteries.   (T) (F)

3. At Yi Peng, there is a parade and there are fireworks.   (T) (F)

4. There is only one lantern in the sky at the Yi Peng festival.   (T) (F)

5. Both the Day of the Dead and the festival of Yi Peng are usually celebrated in November.   (T) (F)

3 Read. Complete the chart.

	Day of the Dead	**Yi Peng**
When is it?		
Why do they celebrate it?		
What do people do?		

4 Work with a partner. Look at the photographs. What do you see? What do you like?

> I like the lanterns. I think they are beautiful.

> I like the lanterns, too! And did you see those skulls?

63

WRITING

1 **Read.** What title does Hiro use for his writing? A title tells you what you are reading about. It's usually short and simple. In the body text of this description, Hiro uses words that describe what he saw, heard, and did.

The Sapporo Snow Festival
by Hiro

Every year we have a snow festival. It's in February, in the winter. This year the festival was fantastic. There was a lot to do, and we had so much fun.

I went to the festival with my brother and sister. It was very cold! I wore a snowsuit, boots, gloves, and a hat. We saw some beautiful snow sculptures. My favorite was a sculpture of two big dinosaurs. They looked so real and so scary!

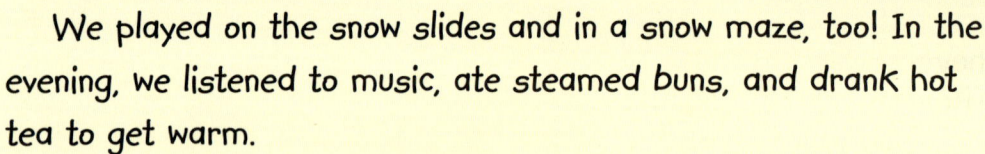

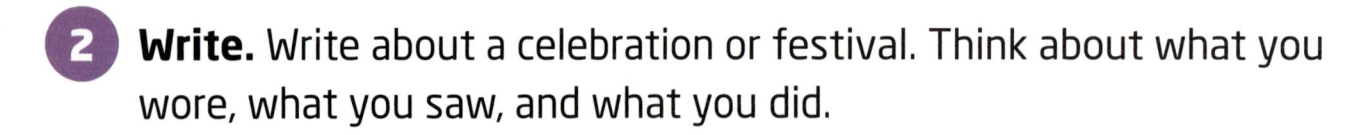

We played on the snow slides and in a snow maze, too! In the evening, we listened to music, ate steamed buns, and drank hot tea to get warm.

2 **Write.** Write about a celebration or festival. Think about what you wore, what you saw, and what you did.

3 **Share your writing.** Work in a small group. Listen and fill in the chart.

Name	Celebration or festival	What did people see and do?

VALUES

Celebrate your culture.
Enjoy your traditions and festivals.

Think. Pair. Share.
How do you celebrate your culture?

San Sosti, Italy

PROJECT

Make a parade mask.
Decorate it and describe it to the class.

1 Choose a celebration.

2 Do research.

3 Collect materials.

4 Decorate your mask.

Now I can . . .

○ talk about celebrations and festivals.

○ tell what happened in the past.

○ talk about cultural traditions.

I made the eyes with white, blue, and yellow paper.

Unit 9

My Weekend

In this unit, I will . . .
- talk about free-time activities.
- talk about the past.
- talk about hobbies.

Look and check.

The boys are
- ○ playing basketball.
- ○ playing volleyball.
- ○ playing soccer.

They are
- ○ tired.
- ○ happy.
- ○ bored.

Chefchaouen, Morocco

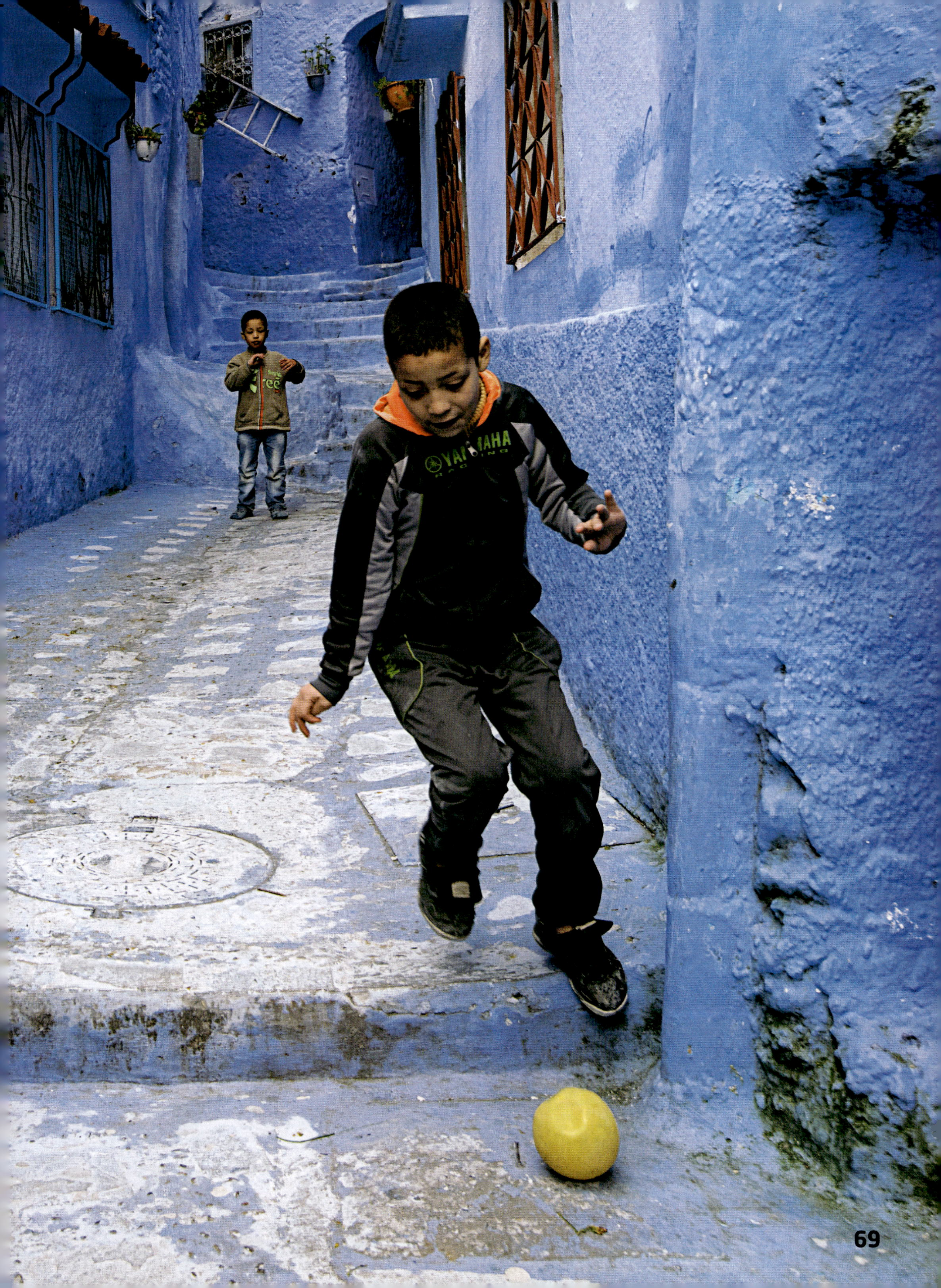

VOCABULARY 1

1 **Listen and read.** TR: 9.1

2 **Listen and say.** TR: 9.2

The weekend is a time to relax and do fun things. Sometimes we stay home. Other times we go out and visit places, play outside, or see friends.

eat out

go to the movies

visit a museum

go on a picnic

stay home

go to the beach

Cabo San Lucas, Mexico

lose

win

exciting

interesting

text my friends

busy

3 **Ask and answer.** Work with a partner.

What do you do on weekends?

Sometimes I go to the movies. How about you?

71

SONG

1 Listen. Read and sing. TR: 9.3

Free Time

Free time, free time, free time is great.
There is no school, and I can sleep late.
In my free time I like to have fun.
I throw and catch. I jump and run.

CHORUS
What did you do on your weekend?
Did you stay at home? Did you have some fun?
What did you do on your weekend?
Did you go outside and play in the sun?

Did you go fishing?
Did you play baseball?
Did you go walking?
What did you do?

Did you go swimming?
Did you go hiking?
Did you go horseback riding?

Bajau boys swimming

I didn't go fishing or walking.
I didn't go swimming or hiking.
I played a game with my little brother.
I went to the movies with
my mother.

CHORUS

Did you go fishing?
Did you play baseball?
Did you go walking?
What did you do?

Did you go swimming?
Did you go hiking?
Did you go horseback riding?

I stayed at home.
I played with everyone.
I lost at baseball, but it was fun.
I texted friends. I helped cook dinner.
When I help out, I feel like a winner.

CHORUS

Free time, free time, free time is great.
There is no school, and I can sleep late.
In my free time I like to have fun.
I dance and sing. I play and run.

2 Talk. Work with a partner.

1. What three things from the song do you do in your free time?

2. What three things from the song don't you do in your free time?

GRAMMAR 1

Simple past: *wh-* questions and negative TR: 9.4

How was your weekend? It was boring. I **didn't do** anything special.
What did you do? I went to a soccer game.
Did your team win? No, they **didn't win.** They lost.

1 **Read and write.** Complete the sentences. Use these words.

didn't eat out   didn't go   didn't watch   didn't win   went   won

What did you do on the weekend?

1. We _____ on a picnic because it was raining!

2. We _____ to the movies. We saw a great movie.

3. We played basketball on Saturday. We _____. We lost!

4. On Sunday we had lunch at home. We _____.

5. Monday we didn't eat out. We _____ on a picnic.

6. Last weekend we _____ to the beach. The weather was bad.

7. Yesterday I _____ TV. I played video games.

8. I went to the game. It was great! We _____!

2 **Write.** Write about things you did and didn't do on the weekend.

Things I did

1. _____
2. _____
3. _____
4. _____

Things I didn't do

5. _____
6. _____
7. _____
8. _____

3 **Ask and answer.** Work with a partner.

How was your weekend?

It was boring!

Why?

I didn't go to the movies. I didn't eat out. I stayed home.

VOCABULARY 2

1 **Listen and say.** Read and write. TR: 9.5

go horseback riding

go fishing

go hiking

go swimming

go ice skating

1. I _____ in winter. I can go fast on the ice.

2. I _____ with my Dad. We don't catch many fish!

3. I _____ sometimes. Horses can run very fast.

4. I _____ with my family. We go into the woods.

5. I _____ every weekend. I can swim very well now.

2 **Stick your favorite activities.** Work with a partner. Ask and answer.

Do you want to go mountain climbing?

No, I don't. I want to go hiking.

1   2   3   4   5

GRAMMAR 2

go + verb + -ing TR: 9.6

What **do** you **do** on weekends?
What **did** you **do** last weekend?

We usually **go hiking**.
We **didn't go hiking**.
We **went swimming**.

1 **Look and write.**

What did Carlos do on the weekend?

1. He went ice skating.
2. _____
3. _____
4. _____
5. _____

2 **Play a game.** Cut out the game board in the back of the book. Play with a partner. Take turns. Flip a coin.

What did you do last weekend?

Heads: Yes + move one space

Tails: No

I didn't go shopping.

READING

1 **Listen and read.** TR: 9.7

Wow! Look at That!

Museums are great places to visit on the weekend. They teach us about the world in fun ways. Many museums have special exhibitions for children. Other museums are ALL for children!

Are these dinosaurs escaping from a museum? At The Children's Museum in Indianapolis, USA, there are giant models of dinosaurs outside. Some of them are running away, and others are looking in through the window!

In one exhibit, called National Geographic Treasures of the Earth, you can learn a lot about the history of Egypt.

Inside the museum there are real dinosaur fossils, rooms about science, art, culture, history, and much more. You can learn about the stars in the planetarium, you can go to the theater, and you can even go rock climbing!

Weird but true
In Turkey there's a museum of hair. It has hair from more than 16,000 people!

National Geographic Treasures of the Earth

78 Unit 9

This is a map of part of the museum.
What is next to the trains?

- Theater
- Planetarium
- Treasures of the Earth
- Trains
- Dinosaurs

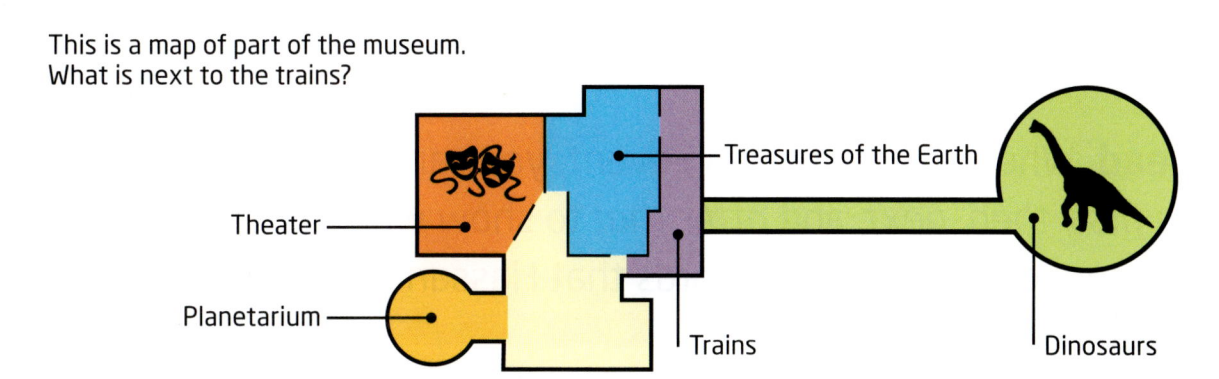

2 **Read.** Match to make sentences.

1. The Children's Museum is
2. The dinosaurs outside of the museum
3. You can learn about the stars
4. There are giant models of dinosaurs
5. You can go to the theater, and you can

a. in the planetarium.
b. in Indianapolis, USA.
c. look like they're running away.
d. go rock climbing.
e. outside the museum.

3 **Read.** What's at the Children's Museum in Indianapolis? Make a chart. Write.

Things I know are there	Things I think are there
Giant models of dinosaurs	

4 **Ask and answer questions.** Talk about museums you know. Take turns.

I went to a toy museum today.

That's interesting! What did you see?

79

WRITING

1 Read. When you describe an event, you can use words such as *first, then, next,* and *after that* to show when things happened. Underline the words that Hassan uses to say when he did things.

My Perfect Weekend

I got up early on Saturday, and it was warm and sunny. First I ate my favorite breakfast—a bowl of yogurt, honey, and nuts! After that I went fishing with my friend Yildiray. We took lunch with us. We were out all day. In the evening I watched TV with my brothers.

On Sunday we didn't get up early. I read my comic book in bed. Next we got ready to see my favorite soccer team. We went to the stadium. My team won, of course! We sang and shouted a lot! It was a fantastic weekend!

2 Write. Describe a good weekend you had. What did you do?

3 Share your writing. Work in a small group. Listen and fill the chart.

Name	What did he or she do?

VALUES

Try new things.
Discover the things you love.

Think. Pair. Share.
Do you like to try new things? Why or why not?

Ice fishing in Hwacheon-gun, South Korea

81

PROJECT

Make a class scrapbook.
Show and tell your favorite activities. Present your work.

1. Take photos or draw pictures of five weekend activities you like.

2. Make a collage of your photos and drawings.

3. Write about your weekend activities.

4. Add your page to the class scrapbook.

"I love picnics. Last weekend I went on a picnic with my family and some friends."

Last weekend, I went on a picnic with my family and friends.

I usually go horseback riding on the weekends.

I went to a soccer game.

I went to the movies with my friend Lorena.

On Sunday I stayed home. I didn't do anything special.

Now I can . . .

- ○ talk about free-time activities.
- ○ talk about the past.
- ○ talk about hobbies.

EXTENDED READING

1 **Listen and read.** TR: 6.9

The Gingerbread Man

Grandma makes a beautiful gingerbread man. "Mmmm. I'm hungry. I want to eat you," says Grandma.

The gingerbread man jumps up. He says, *"You can't eat me! Run, run, as fast as you can. You can't catch me, I'm the gingerbread man!"* Grandma is surprised!

The gingerbread man runs out of the house. Grandma runs after him.

He runs to a forest. He sees a fox. "Mmmm. I'm hungry," says the fox. "I want to eat you!"

The gingerbread man says, *"You can't eat me! Run, run, as fast as you can. You can't catch me. I'm the gingerbread man!"*

He sees a coyote. "Mmmm. I'm hungry," says the coyote. "I want to eat you!" The coyote runs after the gingerbread man.

The gingerbread man says, *"You can't eat me! Run, run, as fast as you can. You can't catch me. I'm the gingerbread man!"*

He runs to a river. He sees a turtle. "I'm not hungry. I don't want to eat you," says the turtle.

"Oh, good!" says the gingerbread man. "I have to cross the river! Can you help me, please?"

"Yes, I can," says the turtle. "Jump on my back."

The gingerbread man jumps on the turtle's back. They swim across the river.

The gingerbread man jumps off the turtle's back. He says, "Thank you," and runs away.

"Run, run, as fast as you can. You can't catch me. I'm the gingerbread man!"

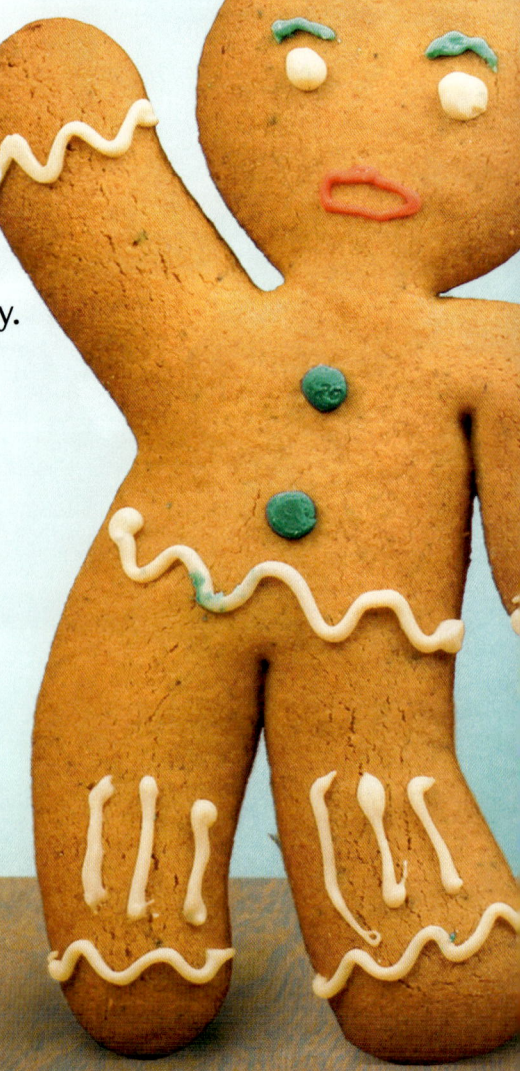

2 Read and match. You can match more than one.

Grandma • runs after the gingerbread man.

fox • is hungry.

coyote • makes a gingerbread man.

turtle • takes the gingerbread man across the river.

3 Read and check. Check **T** for *True* and **F** for *False*.

1. The gingerbread man is a cookie.   T   F
2. The fox doesn't want to eat the gingerbread man.   T   F
3. The turtle helps the gingerbread man.   T   F

4 Express yourself. Choose an activity.

a. Write a short paragraph about what happens to the gingerbread man next.

b. Make masks and perform a play about the gingerbread man.

c. Make or bake your own gingerbread man. Take photos. Share them with your class.

EXTENDED READING

1 **Listen and read.** TR: 9.8

THE Paralympics

You've probably heard of the Olympic Games. People from many countries come together every four years to run, swim, and play other sports at the Olympics. Another great sporting event, called the Paralympic Games, also takes place every four years.

At the Paralympics, people with disabilities come together to run, swim, and compete at sports. Years ago people with disabilities didn't take part in many sports. Now at the Paralympics they compete in sports such as skiing, wheelchair tennis, and judo. At the beginning of the Games they dress in their national uniforms and take part in parades. When they win, they receive medals that celebrate their strength.

Daniel Dias was born with no hands and only one foot. In school, children called him names. He stayed home a lot. He didn't do much. When he was 16, Daniel watched the Paralympics on TV and saw disabled people like him swimming. He exercised and learned to swim. Soon he was fit and strong. He was also very fast. He won gold medals in his first Paralympic Games in Beijing.

The Paralympic Games changed Daniel's life. They are also helping to change how people see Paralympians and other people with physical disabilities.

2 **Write.** Complete the sentences with words from the box.

| disabilities   four   medals   parade   swim |

a. The Olympics and the Paralympics take place every _____ years.

b. Paralympians are athletes who also have _____ .

c. At the beginning of the Paralympics, there is a _____ .

d. After he saw the Paralympics, Daniel Dias learned to _____ .

3 **Read.** Write a list of Paralympic sports from the text. Can you think of more? Work with a partner.

4 **Express yourself.** Choose an activity.

a. Learn about a Paralympian from your country. Tell the class about him or her.

b. Pretend that you are a journalist and your partner is Daniel Dias. Act out an interview with him.

c. Make a poster about the Paralympics.

Unit 5
Animal Habitats

VOCABULARY 1

1 **Look and match.** Write the number.

- ○ a hive
- ○ an island
- ○ grasslands
- ○ a web
- ○ underground
- ○ snow
- ○ ice
- ○ wetlands
- ○ a rain forest
- ○ a forest
- ○ a nest
- ○ a cave
- ○ a desert
- ○ mud

2 Look at the pictures. Read and write.

1. What's the hippo playing in? _____

2. What's the iceberg made of? _____

3. Where do trees grow? _____

SONG

1. Listen to the song. Read. Draw lines to match. TR: 5.1

1. Why does a giraffe have a long neck?
2. Why does a frog have strong legs?
3. Why does a polar bear have white fur?

a. Because it lives in ice and snow.
b. Because it eats leaves at the tops of the trees.
c. Because it hops, swims, and jumps.

2. Write a new verse for the song. Use words from the box. Draw a picture for your verse.

climbs trees	a crocodile	eats meat	hops
a kangaroo	a lion	a monkey	sharp claws
sharp teeth	strong arms	strong legs	swings in trees
a tiger			

Why does _____ have _____?

Why? Why?

Because it _____

_____

_____.

90   Unit 5

GRAMMAR 1

Why . . . ?/Because . . .

Question				Answer		
Why	do	snakes	come out during the day?	Because	they	like the sun.
	don't	you	like crocodiles?		they	are scary.
	can	frogs	jump high?		they	have strong legs.
	can't	birds	climb trees?		they	don't have arms.

1 **Read and write.** Use words from the box.

> are   Because   do   does   don't   is   Why

1. __Why don't__ fish run?
   __Because__ they don't have legs.

2. _____ hippos stand in water?
   _____ the sun is hot, and hippos feel cool in the water.

3. _____ the parrot eating a nut?
   _____ parrots like nuts.

4. _____ the desert dry?
   _____ there is very little rain in the desert.

5. _____ the birds in the wetlands?
   _____ they eat frogs and fish, and frogs and fish live in the wetlands.

6. _____ the tiger drink water?
   _____ it is thirsty.

7. _____ zebras live underground?
   _____ zebras eat grass, and there isn't any grass underground.

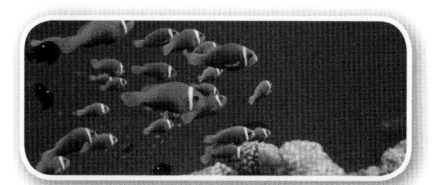

2 **Read and match.** Draw lines.

1. Why is the rabbit going underground?
2. Why don't penguins live on grasslands?
3. Why are the zebras running?
4. Why are the elephants in the water?
5. Why is the bird flying to the nest?

a. Because they are taking a bath.
b. Because its home is underground.
c. Because penguins need to eat fish and food in the ocean.
d. Because its babies are in the nest.
e. Because they see a lion, and they are scared.

3 **Write.** What do you like? What don't you like? Work with a partner. Read your partner's sentences. Ask your partner questions. Use words from the box.

caves	forests
grasslands	hives
ice	islands
mud	rain forests
snow	webs

I like rain forests.

Why do you like rain forests?

Because I like monkeys and parrots, and they live in rain forests.

I like _____.

I don't like _____.

92   Unit 5

VOCABULARY 2

1 **Listen and write.** Use words from the box. TR: 5.2

fur   horns   pouch   tongue   wings

1. A kangaroo has a _____.
2. A butterfly has _____. It can fly.
3. A frog has a long, sticky _____.
4. A goat has two _____ on its head.
5. A lion has _____.

2 **Look and read.** Check **T** for *True* or **F** for *False*.

1. A giraffe has a long tongue.　　T　F
2. A cow has a pouch.　　T　F
3. A chicken has wings.　　T　F
4. A panda has black and white fur.　　T　F
5. A donkey has horns.　　T　F

GRAMMAR 2

Infinitive of purpose

Parrots			wings	**to fly**.	
Cats	use	their	tongues	**to clean**	their fur.
Kangaroos			pouches	**to carry**	their babies.

1 Listen and write. TR: 5.3

> to carry   to clean   to eat   to fight   to fly
> to hide   to jump   to protect   to run   to swim

1. Goats use their horns _____.
2. Polar bears use their white fur _____ in the ice and snow.
3. Lions use their teeth _____ meat.
4. Horses use their legs _____.
5. Ostriches use their legs _____ fast.
6. Giraffes use their long tongues _____ their eyes.
7. Tigers use their mouths _____ their babies.
8. Penguins use their wings _____.
9. Cats use their sharp claws _____ their babies.
10. Owls use their wings _____.

2 What about you? What do you use? Write.

1. What do you use to eat? _____
2. What do you use to walk? _____
3. What do you use to write? _____

3 Work with a partner. Student 1, go to page 149. Student 2, go to page 150. Read. listen, and talk. Take turns.

94 Unit 5

GAME TIME!

1 Read the clues. Do the puzzle.

1. Why can a frog catch a fly with its _____? Because it is sticky.
2. Why can't a zebra fly? Because it doesn't have _____.
3. Goats use their _____ to fight.
4. Why does an owl have big eyes? _____ it needs to see at night.
5. Many turtles live in _____.
6. Lions live in _____.
7. Camels live in the _____.
8. Big spiders live in the _____.

1. GEONUT
2. GIWSN
3. HONRS
4. CEABESU
5. LATDENSW
6. GAASLRDNSS
7. RETSED
8. IRNA SROFTE

2 Listen and read. Can you say these fast? TR: 5.4

1. My nephew never stands next to a nest.
2. We walk through the wetlands in windy weather.
3. Do the polar bear and panda play in the park?

READING

1 **Listen and read.** TR: 5.5

The Coolest Animals Live in Antarctica!

Antarctica is very cold, very dry, and very windy. Can animals live there? Yes, they can!

The emperor penguin is a bird. It can't fly, but it can swim. The mother penguin lays an egg on the ice. Where is the nest for this egg? The father emperor penguin takes care of the egg. He puts it on his feet! Why? Because he can keep the egg warm.

The Weddell seal lives in Antarctica, too. It spends a lot of time in the ocean. It can stay underwater for forty-five minutes. The seal swims under the ice. Why? Because it catches fish and eats underwater. It is safe under the ice.

The Arctic tern is a small but amazing bird. It lives in Antarctica in the winter and flies to the Arctic in the summer! Why do the terns fly to the Arctic? Because the birds make nests there. The nests are on the ground. The mother lays eggs in the nest. The parents protect their nest and their babies. The parents feed the young birds, too.

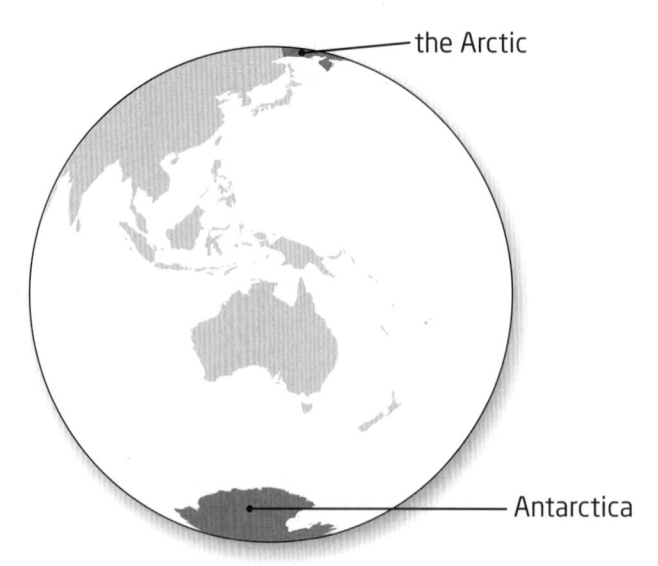

the Arctic

Antarctica

emperor penguin

Weddell seal

Arctic tern

96 Unit 5

2 Read. Check T for *True* or F for *False*.

1. The emperor penguin can swim well.   T   F
2. The emperor penguin father takes care of the egg.   T   F
3. The Weddell seal can swim under the ice.   T   F
4. Antarctica is hot and sunny.   T   F
5. The Arctic tern flies to the Arctic in the summer.   T   F

3 Complete the chart. Then work with a partner. Talk about animals in Antarctica.

Animal	What can it do?	More information
emperor penguin	The _____ lays an egg on the ice. The father takes care of the egg.	The _____ puts the egg on his feet. He keeps the egg warm.
_____	It spends a lot of time in the ocean.	It can swim under the ice. It eats _____.
Arctic tern	It flies between _____ _____.	It lives _____ in the winter. It flies to the Arctic in the summer. It builds a nest and lays eggs in the Arctic.

4 Read and write.

1. The father emperor penguin takes care of the _____.
2. The Weddell seal can swim under the _____.
3. The Arctic tern flies between _____ and the Arctic.
4. The Arctic tern builds a _____ in the Arctic.

Weird but true

Polar bears live in the Arctic.
A polar bear's fur is white, but its skin is black!

WRITING

1 **Read.** Underline the words that tell what the animal looks like and what the animal does. Write the name of the animal.

It lives in grasslands. It is brown and yellow. It can run. It has long legs and a long neck. It eats leaves at the tops of trees. It uses its long tongue to clean its eyes and ears.

What is it?

It's a _____.

2 **Draw a picture of an animal.** Describe it. Tell where it lives. Tell what it looks like. Tell what it does. Then work with a partner. Read your description and ask, "What is the animal?"

This animal lives _____. It is _____.

It can _____. It has _____.

It eats _____. It uses its _____ to _____.

98 Unit 5

UNIT 5 REVIEW

1 **Look at the picture.** Circle the hive, the cave, the web, the mud, and the nest.

2 **Look at the picture.** Read and write. Use words from the box.

| Because | to eat | a forest | fur | grasslands | to hop |
| nest | to see | snow | wetlands | Why | wings |

1. The animals live in _____.
2. A butterfly uses its _____ to fly.
3. The rabbit has soft _____.
4. The rabbit uses its legs _____.
5. The turtle uses its eyes _____.
6. _____ is one bear big? Because it's the mother.
7. Why is one bear small? _____ it's a baby bear.
8. The bird is in the _____.

99

Unit 6
What's for Dinner?

VOCABULARY 1

1 Listen and write. TR: 6.1

| a bag | a bottle | a bowl | a box | a bunch |
| a can | a glass | a jar | a loaf | a piece |

1. _a bag_ of rice (g)
2. _____ of cake ( )
3. _____ of sugar ( )
4. _____ of oil ( )
5. _____ of olives ( )
6. _____ of soda ( )
7. _____ of bananas ( )
8. _____ of juice ( )
9. _____ of cereal ( )
10. _____ of bread ( )

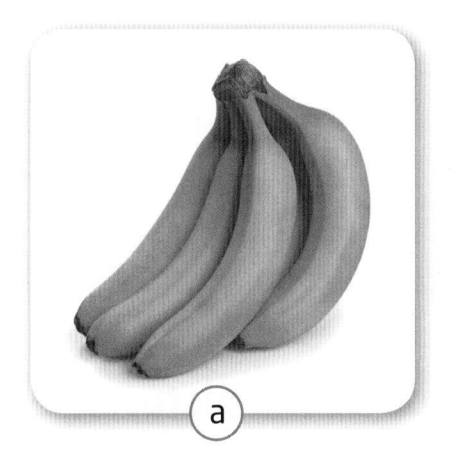

a

b

100 Unit 6

2 **Read the words in Activity 1.** Look at the pictures. Match.
Write the letters in the circles next to the words.

SONG

1 **Listen to the song.** Look at the pictures. Read. Check ✓ the box when you hear the word. TR: 6.2

a bowl of rice

a bowl of ice cream

a bowl of pasta

a can of soda

a glass of milk

bread

a cake

a cookie

2 **Listen and write.** TR: 6.3

1. A jar of jelly is no fun,
   if there isn't any _____ to spread it on.
   _____ is very nice,
   but it tastes better with some spice.

2. _____, a jar of spice,
   _____, and _____ are nice!
   Let's go now. Let's buy some food.
   Let's go shopping, just me and you!

102 Unit 6

GRAMMAR 1

some and **any**

Question				Answer						
Are	there	**any**	eggs?	Yes,	there	are	**some**	on the table.	aren't = are not
			apples?	No,	there	aren't	**(any)**.		
Is	there	**any**	cheese?	Yes,	there	is	**some**	in the fridge.	isn't = is not
			rice?	No,	there	isn't	**(any)**.		

1 Listen. Read and (circle). TR: 6.4

1. Is there any cake?
   Yes, there is some.   No, there isn't any.
2. Are there any bottles of oil?
   Yes, there are some.   No, there aren't any.
3. Are there any pieces of cake?
   Yes, there are some.   No, there aren't any.
4. Is there any cereal?
   Yes, there is some.   No, there isn't any.

2 Look at the picture. Read and write.

1. Are there ____any____ beans?
   Yes, there are some in a jar.

2. Are there _____ cans of soda?
   _____

3. Is there _____ orange juice?
   _____

4. Are there _____ eggs?
   _____

5. Are there _____ bottles of apple juice?

3 **Circle five foods.** Draw them. Answer the questions. Use *any* or *some* in your answers. Then work with a partner. Don't show your picture. Your partner asks questions about your picture.

bags of rice	bags of sugar	bottles of milk
bottles of oil	boxes of cereal	boxes of noodles
bunches of bananas	bunches of grapes	cans of soda
jars of olives	loaves of bread	pieces of cake

1. Are there any bunches of bananas? _____

2. Is there any bread? _____

3. Are there any olives? _____

4. Is there any oil? _____

5. Are there any boxes of noodles? _____

Are there any bags of sugar?

No, there aren't any.

Is there any cereal?

Yes, there is some.

104　Unit 6

VOCABULARY 2

1 **Listen and read.** Write. TR: 6.5

1. The _____ of that hamburger is ninety-nine cents.
2. Let's _____ the milk and eggs in the refrigerator.
3. I'm hungry. Let's go to the supermarket and _____ some food.
4. Which is better, yogurt or ice cream? Let's _____ them.
5. Oh no! I don't have any _____! I can't take the bus home.

2 **Read and write.** Use words from the box. Use some words more than one time.

> buy   compare   money   price   put away

1. I'm thirsty. Let's _____ a can of soda.
2. The _____ of that bag of nuts is fifty cents.
3. I have twenty cents. Do you have any _____?
4. Yes, I have some _____.
5. I have ninety cents. We can _____ a bag of nuts and a can of soda.
6. Which snack is better for me? I need to _____ them.
7. I _____ my toys after I play with them.

105

GRAMMAR 2

a few and a little

Question				Answer					
Are	there	any	nuts?	Yes,	there	are	**a few**	on the table.	aren't = are not
			olives?	No,	there	aren't	(any).		
Is	there	any	juice?	Yes,	there	is	**a little**	in the bottle.	isn't = is not
			tea?	No,	there	isn't	(any).		

1 **Read.** Write the foods in the correct columns in the chart.

> bunches of bananas   hamburgers   ice cream   loaves of bread   milk
> potatoes   salad   sandwiches   soup

There are a few	There is a little
bunches of bananas	milk

2 **Read and write.** Use *is a little* or *are a few*.

1. Are there any bags of rice? Yes, there _____.
2. Are there any boxes of cereal? Yes, there _____.
3. Is there any oil in the bottle? Yes, there _____.
4. Is there any pasta in the bowl? Yes, there _____.
5. Are there any cans of soda? Yes, there _____.
6. Is there any sugar in the bowl? Yes, there _____.
7. Is there any cake? Yes, there _____.

3 **Work with a partner.** Student 1, go to page 148. Student 2, go to page 151. Read. listen, and talk. Take turns.

GAME TIME!

1 **Write.** Answer the questions about your classroom. Use sentences from the box. Then check your answers with a partner.

> Yes, there are a few.   Yes, there are some.   Yes, there is a little.
> Yes, there is some.   No, there aren't any. No, there isn't any.

1. Is there any water? _____
2. Are there any bags? _____
3. Is there any soda? _____
4. Is there any glue? _____
5. Are there any snacks? _____
6. Are there any windows? _____

2 **Look at the pictures.** Circle the words.

h	k	d	p	r	i	c	e
c	s	x	y	q	g	p	a
m	o	z	c	w	t	p	j
q	a	m	z	x	s	w	b
e	f	v	p	b	g	t	u
p	u	t	★	a	w	a	y
y	j	m	i	k	r	l	u
o	p	l	m	o	n	e	y

3 **Listen and read.** Can you say these fast? TR: 6.6

1. Put away the pasta, peppers, and potatoes.

2. Betty buys a big bunch of bananas.

3. Compare the cheese, chips, and chicken carefully.

107

READING

1 Listen and read. TR: 6.7

Special Food

Making Chinese dumplings for the New Year

People around the world eat different food. People in many places eat special food on holidays. In China, people make dumplings for the New Year. People in Japan eat noodles called *soba*. Some people think eating soba noodles on the New Year is lucky.

In Italy and Poland, people eat bread for Christmas. In Poland, people eat sweet bread called *babka*. In Italy, people eat a sweet bread called *panettone*. Sometimes the bread has fruit or honey.

People also eat special food for birthdays. In the United States, people eat cake. But people in Korea eat seaweed soup. What special food do you eat?

Japanese soba noodles

2 Read. Check T for *True* or F for *False*.

1. All people eat the same food. T F
2. Babka are noodles from Poland. T F
3. People in Italy eat dumplings for the New Year. T F
4. Some people think eating soba noodles on the New Year is lucky. T F

3 Read and write.

1. What do people in Poland eat on Christmas?

   _____

2. When do people in Korea eat seaweed soup?

   _____

3. Where do people eat dumplings on the New Year?

   _____

4 Do you eat special foods? Complete the chart. Work with a partner.

	Birthday	New Year	Holidays
You			
Your partner			

Weird but true

A chimpanzee eats a birthday cake.

WRITING

1 **Read.** Answer the questions. Write.

My Favorite Birthday Food

Tacos are my favorite birthday food. I love corn tacos filled with spicy meat, fish, or chicken. I like tomatoes and vegetables in my tacos. I eat tacos with my hands! Tacos are fun to eat. They taste delicious, too!

1. Underline the topic sentence of the paragraph.
2. Do the other sentences give more information about the topic, or main idea? _____

2 **Write and draw.** What is your favorite birthday food? Write about it. First write a sentence to tell the topic, or main idea. Write other sentences to tell more about your favorite birthday food. Draw a picture of your favorite birthday food.

_____

_____

_____

_____

110   Unit 6

UNIT 6 REVIEW

1 **Look at the photos.** Write questions and answers. Use words from the box.

Are there any . . .	Yes, there are some. Yes, there are a few. No, there aren't any.
Is there any . . .	Yes, there is some. Yes, there is a little. No, there isn't any.

1. _____ bottles of oil? _____

2. _____ milk? _____

3. _____ sugar? _____

4. _____ boxes of cereal? _____

5. _____ glasses of juice? _____

2 **Read and write.** What about you?

1. Where do you use money? _____

2. What do you like to buy? _____

3. What do you compare? _____

4. Do you put away your clothes and toys? _____

III

Unit 7
Feeling Fit

VOCABULARY 1

1 Look and write.

a back	a knee
a chest	a shoulder
an elbow	a stomach
fingers	toes

2 Circle the best answer.

1. I have ten **knees / elbows / fingers**.

2. I have two **shoulders / toes / backs**.

3. I have one **knee / muscle / stomach**.

4. I can bend my **bone / knees / chest**.

5. I can stretch my **knees / muscles / elbows**.

SONG

1 Listen to the song. Read. Draw lines to match. TR: 7.1

1. Did you stretch your ——————— a. back?
2. Did you move your   b. sleep?
3. Did you get enough   c. legs?
4. Did you eat a healthy   d. snack?
5. Did you stretch your   e. nose?
6. Did you touch your   f. muscles?
7. Did you bend your   g. knees?
8. Did you wiggle your   h. toes?

2 Write a new verse for the song. Use words from the box.

> chest   elbows   fingers   shoulders   stomach

Did you bend your _____? Yes, I did!

Did you move your _____? I did that a lot.

Did you touch your _____? No, I forgot!

Did you stretch your _____? Yes, I did.

GRAMMAR 1

Simple past: Yes/No questions and short answers

Question				Answer							
Did	you	**brush**	your	teeth?	Yes,	I	**did**.	No,	I	**didn't**.	didn't = did not
	he	**make**	his	bed?		he			he		
	they	**do**	their	homework?		they			they		

1 Listen and write. TR: 7.2

1. _____ you _____ your knees?

   Yes, I _____.

2. _____ she _____ in the park?

   Yes, she _____.

3. _____ you _____ breakfast?

   No, I _____.

4. _____ he _____ his back?

   No, he _____.

5. _____ they _____ their homework?

   No, they _____.

2 Listen and match. Draw lines. TR: 7.3

1. Did he walk to school?   a. Yes, I did.
2. Did you play baseball yesterday?   b. Yes, he did.
3. Did he brush his teeth after breakfast? c. No, I didn't.
4. Did you play with friends yesterday?   d. No, he didn't.

3 **Look, read, and write.** Use *did* or *didn't* in your answers.

1. Did she throw the ball? _____Yes, she did._____

2. Did he catch the ball? _____

3. Did the children ride their bikes to the park? _____

4. Did they eat the bread? _____

4 **Write questions.** Then ask your partner. Write the answers.

> Did you eat yogurt for breakfast?

> No, I didn't.

1. Did you __eat yogurt for breakfast__? _____

2. Did you _____? _____

3. Did you _____? _____

4. Did you _____? _____

5. Did you _____? _____

116   Unit 7

VOCABULARY 2

1 **Read and match.** Draw lines to match.

1. I eat vegetables at dinner.
2. I eat junk food on Saturday.
3. I eat fruit every morning.
4. I get rest every day.
5. I get exercise every day.
6. She eats fruit every day.
7. He eats junk food at night.
8. Why does he eat vegetables?
9. Does the baby get rest?
10. She gets exercise every day.

a. I like bananas and oranges.
b. I go to bed at 8:00.
c. I skateboard and rollerblade.
d. I love cookies and ice cream.
e. I like corn and peppers.
f. Because he loves them!
g. She loves mangoes.
h. She swims every afternoon.
i. He eats three bags of chips.
j. Yes. She sleeps at night.

2 **Look, read, and write.** Use words from the box.

> eat fruit   eat vegetables   eats junk food   get exercise   gets rest

1. They _____ every day.
2. They _____ every day. 
3. He _____ every day. 
4. She _____ every day. 

117

GRAMMAR 2

too and enough

too much/too many				enough			
I	eat	**too**	**much**	junk food.	I	don't	eat	**enough**	vegetables.
I	work	**too**	**many**	hours.	I		get	**enough**	exercise.

1 **Read.** Write *too* or *enough*.

1. Don't stay up _____ late!

2. I play soccer every day.
   I get _____ exercise.

3. Don't watch _____ much TV!

4. I drink _____ much soda.

2 **Read and write.** Answer the questions. Check ✓ *Yes* or *No*.

	Yes	No
1. Do you eat too much junk food?		
2. Do you get enough sleep at night?		
3. Do you play too many video games?		
4. Do you drink enough water every day?		
5. Do you eat enough fruit every day?		
6. Do you eat enough vegetables every day?		

GAME TIME!

1 **Work with a partner.** Student 1, go to page 149. Student 2, go to page 150. Take turns.

2 **Do the word puzzle.**

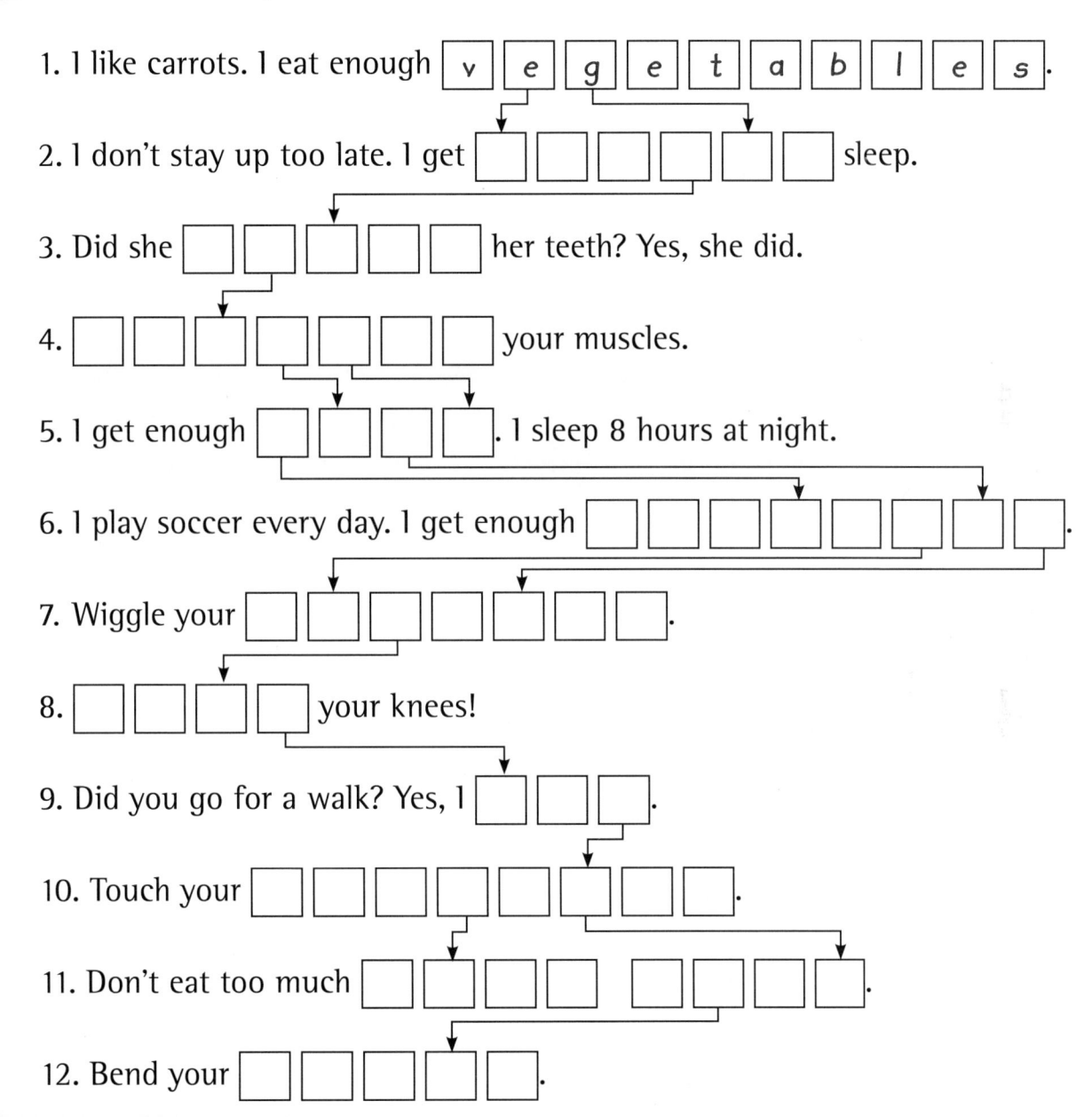

1. I like carrots. I eat enough `v e g e t a b l e s`.
2. I don't stay up too late. I get ☐☐☐☐☐ sleep.
3. Did she ☐☐☐☐☐ her teeth? Yes, she did.
4. ☐☐☐☐☐☐☐ your muscles.
5. I get enough ☐☐☐☐. I sleep 8 hours at night.
6. I play soccer every day. I get enough ☐☐☐☐☐☐☐☐.
7. Wiggle your ☐☐☐☐☐☐.
8. ☐☐☐☐ your knees!
9. Did you go for a walk? Yes, I ☐☐☐.
10. Touch your ☐☐☐☐☐☐☐.
11. Don't eat too much ☐☐☐☐ ☐☐☐☐.
12. Bend your ☐☐☐☐☐.

3 **Listen and read.** Can you say these fast? TR: 7.4

1. Slowly stretch your stomach and shoulders on Sunday.
2. Eat enough fresh fruit every Friday.
3. Bonnie bends her beautiful back.

READING

1 Listen and read. TR: 7.5

Do Animals Need Exercise?

Do animals get enough exercise? Wild animals do. They move a lot to look for food. They run, swim, climb trees, and walk far. Sometimes wild elephants walk more than 27 miles (45 kilometers) a day!

Sometimes animals in zoos don't get enough exercise. They live in small spaces. Zookeepers always feed them. Many zookeepers help animals get exercise. At many zoos, the zookeepers teach elephants to stretch and bend. The elephants walk and run. They lift a heavy ball with their trunk. The zookeepers help big cats, like lions and tigers, too. A zookeeper hides a bone in a tree. Then the zookeeper teaches the big cats to climb and jump to get the bone. Big cats can also play with toys to stretch their muscles.

Sometimes pets don't get enough exercise. Dogs need to run outside. Cats need balls to hit with their paws. Birds need to flap their wings. It's important for pets to get enough exercise. Pet owners need to play with their pets. Exercise helps keep animals fit and healthy.

Weird but true An elephant's trunk can pick up one piece of grass, but it can also lift a big log.

2 Read. Check **T** for *True* or **F** for *False*.

1. Wild animals get enough exercise. T F
2. Big cats pick up balls with their trunks. T F
3. Animals in zoos always get enough exercise. T F
4. Elephants in the wild walk a lot. T F
5. Exercise helps keep pets healthy. T F

3 Read and write. Complete the chart.

Animals and Exercise

	Do animals get enough exercise?	How do animals get exercise?
wild animals	_____	They move a lot to look for food. They run, _____, _____, and _____.
zoo animals	sometimes	Zookeepers help animals get exercise. They teach elephants to _____ and _____ and lift a heavy ball. They teach big cats to _____ and _____ to get bones. Big cats play with toys.
pets	_____	Pet owners _____. Dogs _____. Cats need to play with balls. Birds _____.

4 Read and write.

1. Why do wild animals get enough exercise?

   _____

2. How can zookeepers help elephants get enough exercise?

   _____

3. How can pet owners help their pets get enough exercise?

   _____

WRITING

1 Read and write. Read about Gabriela's favorite vegetable. Underline the sentences with *because*. Write the words that tell why Gabriela likes tomatoes.

Tomatoes Are Great

Tomatoes are my favorite vegetable. <u>I like tomatoes because they are juicy and delicious, and you can eat them hot or cold</u>. You can cook tomatoes to make spaghetti sauce. You can eat them cold in salads. <u>I also like tomatoes because they have beautiful colors</u>! I love red, yellow, orange, and green tomatoes. <u>I also like tomatoes because they help keep you healthy and strong</u>.

_____

_____

_____

2 Write about your favorite vegetable or fruit. Use *because* to explain why you like it.

_____

_____

_____

_____

_____

UNIT 7 REVIEW

1 **Read and write.** Use words from the box.

> Did   didn't   Don't
> enough   exercise   rest   too

1. _____ she eat a snack yesterday? Yes, she did.

2. I get _____ every day. I play basketball.

3. Do you get _____ exercise? No, I watch _____ much TV.

4. Did you do your homework? No, I _____.

5. _____ eat too much junk food.

6. I get _____ every day. I go to sleep at 8:00.

2 **What's important for good health?** Read and check ✓. Then compare your answers with a partner.

	It's important for good health.
Get enough exercise every day.	
Eat fruits and vegetables.	
Eat junk food every day.	
Drink too much soda.	
Stretch your muscles.	
Stay up too late.	
Get enough rest.	
Drink enough water every day.	
Watch too much TV.	
Bend your knees and elbows.	
Eat foods to make your bones strong.	

Unit 8
Let's Celebrate!

VOCABULARY 1

1 Look and write.

| celebrate | a costume | dance | decorations | dress up | a feast |
| fireworks | a lantern | a mask | a parade | a party | remember |

1. _____
2. _____ 
3. _____ 
4. _____ 
5. _____ 
6. _____ 

124   Unit 8

7.  _____ 8.  _____ 9. _____

10.  _____ 11.  _____ 12. _____

2 **Read and circle.** Then compare your answers with a partner.

1. Do you like to dance?   Yes, I do.   No, I don't.
2. Do you like parties?   Yes, I do.   No, I don't.
3. Do you like to wear masks?   Yes, I do.   No, I don't.
4. Do you like to watch parades?   Yes, I do.   No, I don't.
5. Do you like feasts?   Yes, I do.   No, I don't.
6. Do you like decorations?   Yes, I do.   No, I don't.
7. Do you like lanterns?   Yes, I do.   No, I don't.
8. Do you like fireworks?   Yes, I do.   No, I don't.

SONG

1 Listen to the song. Read and write. TR: 8.1

1. We went to a carnival.

   Everyone was there!

   We dressed up, sang some songs,

   and watched a _____.

2. Did you like the food?

   Yes, I liked the food.

   Did you _____?

   Yes, I went as a frog.

3. Did you like the _____?

   Yes, I liked the _____.

   Did you see any _____?

   Yes, we saw some _____.

2 Write a new verse for the song. Use words from the box.

> dances   decorations   feast   fireworks   lanterns   party

Did you like the _____?

Yes, I liked the _____.

Did you see any _____?

Yes, I saw some _____.

126   Unit 8

GRAMMAR 1

Simple past: regular verbs

Question				Answer			
Did	you	watch	the fireworks?	Yes,	we	**watched**	them.
		like	the party?		I	**liked**	it.

1 Listen and write. TR: 8.2

1. _____ you _____ to the party?

2. Yes, we _____ to the party.

3. _____ your cousins _____ with you?

4. Yes, they _____ with me.

5. _____ you _____ the yummy food?

6. Yes, I _____ the yummy food.

2 Read. Match the questions to the answers. Draw lines.

1. Did you listen to music?   a. Yes, I dressed up in a costume.

2. Did you watch fireworks?   b. Yes, I listened to music.

3. Did you dress up in a costume?   c. Yes, we celebrated his birthday.

4. Did you celebrate his birthday?   d. Yes, I liked the feast.

5. Did you like the feast?   e. Yes, we watched fireworks.

6. Did you play games?   f. Yes, we played games.

3 **Write these verbs so they tell about the past.**

1. watch ___watched___
2. listen _____
3. sound _____
4. cook _____

5. taste _____
6. celebrate _____
7. remember _____
8. brush _____

4 **Read and write.**
Complete the sentences. Use verbs from Activity 3.

1. We _____ my brother's birthday yesterday.

2. My grandma _____ noodle soup.

3. The birthday feast _____ delicious.

4. We _____ to music and danced after dinner.

5. After we danced, we _____ a movie on TV.

5 **What did you do on your birthday?** Write. Then talk about what you did with a partner.

I played games on my birthday.

What games did you play?

1. I _____.

2. I _____.

128   Unit 8

VOCABULARY 2

1 **Look and read.** Draw lines to match.

balloons

a birthday cake

candles

a present

2 **Read.** Circle the best answer.

1. Today I'm nine years old. I have nine ____ on my birthday cake.

   a. presents　　　b. invitations　　c. candles

2. My grandpa has ____ to my birthday party.

   a. an invitation　b. a balloon　　　c. a birthday cake

3. I have round ____ as decorations.

   a. presents　　　b. balloons　　　c. invitations

4. My ____ looks sweet and delicious!

   a. candle　　　　b. balloon　　　　c. birthday cake

5. Look at the picture. What's in the paper? It's a big ____ for me.

   a. candle　　　　b. invitation　　　c. present

129

GRAMMAR 2

Simple past: irregular verbs

Question				Answer			
Did	you	wear	a mask?	Yes,	I	**wore**	one.
		buy	her a present?			**bought**	her one.

1 **Look at the gray words.** They are verbs. They change when you talk about the past. Match. Draw lines.

eat	rode	see	wrote
ride	had	write	saw
give	ate	drink	went
have	sang	go	drank
sing	took	wear	made
take	gave	make	wore

2 **Read and write.** Complete the sentences.

1. Did you write the invitations? Yes, I _____ the invitations.

2. Did you wear party hats? Yes, we _____ party hats.

3. Did your friends sing to you? Yes, my friends _____ to me.

4. Did you eat birthday cake? Yes, we _____ birthday cake.

5. Did you have fun? Yes, I _____ fun.

3 **Work with a partner.** Student 1, go to page 148. Student 2, go to page 151. Take turns.

GAME TIME!

1 Read and write. Do the crossword puzzle.

Down

1. I gave him a _____ for his birthday.
4. I don't _____ my third birthday, but I saw photos of it.
5. It was her eighth birthday, and she had eight _____ on her birthday cake.

Across

2. Did your sister wear a mask? Yes, she _____ a mask.
3. Did you sing a song? Yes, I _____ a song.
5. I wore a frog _____ to the party.
6. I saw the _____ in the sky. They were beautiful.
7. Did the children play games? Yes, they _____ games.
8. We _____ my birthday in May.
9. I was thirsty! I _____ the water.

2 Listen and read. Can you say these fast? TR: 8.3

1. Don't dance under the decorations!
2. Please pick up the purple party presents.
3. We celebrated and sang some songs slowly.

READING

1 Listen and read. TR: 8.4

Celebrating the Sun

Many people all over the world celebrate the sun. Sweden is in the north. In winter, nights are long, and days are short. On December 13, people celebrate Lucia Day. It is a festival of lights. People want light on long, dark days! Girls dress up as Lucia. They wear white dresses and wear a candle wreath on their head. Boys dress up as star boys. They wear white clothes and a white hat. They carry stars on sticks. The children sing songs, and people eat cookies and special sweet buns.

In Sweden, the festival of midsummer happens in June. Days are long, and nights are short. People celebrate the longest day of the year and the start of summer. People decorate their homes with flowers and leaves. Many people wear beautiful costumes to the festival. They dance and sing songs. They eat fish, potatoes, fruit, and other foods. People enjoy the sunlight and can forget about the cold, dark winter.

Weird but true

In the north of Sweden, it never gets dark at midsummer.

132 Unit 8

2 Read. Check **T** for *True* or **F** for *False*.

1. Lucia Day is a festival of stars.   T   F
2. Boys dress up as star boys on Lucia Day.   T   F
3. Girls wear candle wreaths on their head on Lucia Day.   T   F
4. The Swedish festival of midsummer is in December.   T   F
5. People dance and sing at the festival of midsummer.   T   F

3 Read. Complete the chart. Then compare your chart with your partner.

	Lucia Day	**Midsummer**
When is it?		
What is it?	It is a festival of lights.	It is a festival to celebrate the longest day of the year and the start of summer.
What do people do?		

4 Read and write.

1. What do girls wear to dress up as Lucia?

_____

2. What special food do people eat on Lucia Day?

_____

3. What do people eat at the midsummer feast?

_____

WRITING

1 **Read.** Write. Answer the questions.

A Thanksgiving Day Parade

By Lisa

Every year there is a big parade in New York City on Thanksgiving Day. Thanksgiving is an American holiday. Last year we were in New York City, and I wanted to see the parade. It was cold, so I wore a warm coat and a hat. The parade was great! I listened to marching bands play music. I watched great dancers. My favorite things were the big balloons shaped like animals!

1. What is the title of Lisa's writing? _____

2. What did Lisa wear? _____

3. What did Lisa hear? _____

4. What did Lisa see? _____

2 **Write about a parade or a party you went to.** Write a title for your paragraph. What did you wear? What did you see? What did you hear? What did you do?

_____

By _____

_____

_____

_____

_____

_____

UNIT 8 REVIEW

1 **Read and draw.**

1. Draw a birthday cake.
2. Draw candles on the cake.
3. Color the candles.
4. Draw a present next to the cake.

2 **Listen and write.** TR: 8.5

1. _____ you _____ to color the candles?
2. Yes, I _____.
3. Yes, I _____ my birthday.
4. Yes, they _____ me a present.
5. Yes, I _____ it.

3 **Read.** Unscramble the sentences. Write.

1. Did / see / you / lanterns?

_____

2. lanterns / I / saw / Yes,

_____

3. wear / Did / a / mask? / you

_____

4. mask / wore / a / I / Yes,

_____

135

Unit 9
My Weekend

VOCABULARY 1

1 **Look and write.** Then ask and answer with a partner.

> eat out   go on a picnic   go to the beach   go to the movies
> stay home   text my friends   visit a museum

1. _____

2. _____

3. _____

4. _____

5. _____

6. _____

Do you eat out on weekends?

Yes, I do.

7. _____

2 Listen and write. Use words from the box. TR: 9.1

busy   exciting   interesting   lose   win

1. I play soccer. I like to _____.

2. I play games. I don't like to _____.

3. The museum was _____.

4. Last weekend, I was _____. I had too much homework!

5. The parade was _____.

SONG

1 **Listen to the song.** Read. Look. Draw lines to match. TR: 9.2

Did you go fishing?

Did you play baseball?

Did you go walking?

Did you go swimming?

Did you go hiking?

Did you go horseback riding?

2 **Listen.** Read and write. TR: 9.3

I _____ _____ fishing or walking.

I didn't _____ swimming or hiking.

I _____ a game with my little brother.

I _____ to the _____ with my mother.

138   Unit 9

GRAMMAR 1

Simple past: wh- questions and negative

Question	Answer					
How was your weekend?	It was boring.			I **didn't** **have** fun.		didn't = did not
What did you do last weekend?	I	**didn't**	**go** out.	I stayed home.		
What did your brother do?	He	**didn't**	**stay** home.	He played in a soccer game.		
Did his team win?	No, they	**didn't**	**win**.	They lost.		

1 Listen and circle. TR: 9.4

1. I went to the movies. / I went to the beach.
2. No, I didn't visit a museum. / Yes, I visited a museum.
3. Yes, I went on a picnic. / No, I didn't go on a picnic.
4. My team didn't win. / My team won.
5. I had an interesting weekend! / I had an exciting weekend!
6. Yes, we went to the movies. / No, we didn't go to the movies.

2 Read and match. Draw lines.

1. How was your weekend?
2. Did your team win?
3. Did you eat out?
4. Did you go to the movies?
5. Did you visit a museum?
6. What did you do on Sunday?

a. No, I didn't go to the movies.
b. It was exciting. I went to the zoo.
c. No, they didn't win. They lost.
d. Yes, I did. I saw 100 paintings!
e. I flew in a helicopter.
f. No, we didn't eat out. We ate pizza at home.

3 **Read and write.** Complete the sentences. Use words from the box.

> didn't lose   didn't stay   didn't text   didn't win
> stayed   texted   visited   won

1. I _____ a museum. It was interesting.
2. I played soccer, but my team _____. I was sad.
3. My family didn't eat out. We _____ home and ate dinner.
4. I texted my friend, but he was busy and _____ me back.
5. My brother _____ home after dinner. He went to the movies.

4 **Read and write.** What about you? What did you do on the weekend? Compare your answers with a partner.

1. Did you fly in a helicopter? (fly → flew)

   Yes, I flew in a helicopter.

2. Did you do your homework?

   _____

3. Did you go on a picnic?

   _____

4. Did you stay home?

   _____

5. Did you text your friends?

   _____

6. Did you lose a game? (lose → lost)

   _____

VOCABULARY 2

1 **Look, read, and match.** Write the letter.

1. I go fishing in the river near my house. _____
2. My family likes to go hiking. _____
3. I go horseback riding on weekends. _____
4. I go ice skating in very cold weather. _____
5. I go swimming on hot days. _____

2 **Read and write.** Use words from the box.

| go fishing | go hiking | go horseback riding |
| go ice skating | go swimming | |

1. I _____ at the swimming pool in summer.
2. You have a horse! Do you _____?
3. It is very cold! I can _____.
4. I want fish for dinner. Let's _____.
5. I wear shoes and socks to _____. I walk and climb.

141

GRAMMAR 2

go + verb + -ing

Question					Answer		
What	do / did	you	do	on the weekend?	I	go	swimming.
						went	hiking.
					I	didn't go	shopping.
What	does / did	she	do	on the weekend?	She	goes	swimming.
						went	hiking.
					She	didn't go	shopping.

1 **Look, read, and write.** Use *go* or *went* in your answers.

1. What did Mai do last weekend?
   She _____.

2. What did her brother do last weekend?
   He _____.
   What didn't Mai do?
   She _____.

3. What did Ivan do last weekend?
   He _____.

4. What did his sister do last weekend?
   She _____.
   What didn't Ivan do?
   He _____.

GAME TIME!

1 Listen and read. (Circle.) TR: 9.5

1. Olivia went horseback riding.   Olivia didn't go horseback riding.
2. She went bike riding.   She didn't go bike riding.
3. Olivia went skateboarding.   Olivia didn't go skateboarding.
4. Olivia went ice skating.   Olivia didn't go ice skating.
5. She went swimming.   She didn't go swimming.

2 Work with a partner. Student 1, go to page 149. Student 2, go to page 150. Take turns.

3 Look, read, and write. Answer the questions.

Monica   Miguel   Elena   Luis

1. What did Monica do on the weekend? She _____.
2. What did Luis do last weekend? He _____.
3. Did Elena go horseback riding? No, _____.
4. What did Elena do? She _____.
5. Miguel usually goes to the beach on weekends. What did Miguel do last weekend?

   He _____.

4 Listen and read. Can you say these fast? TR: 9.6

1. Why did we win the weekend game?
2. She went swimming and shopping on Saturday.
3. Bobby is busy at the beach.

READING

1 Listen and read. TR: 9.7

Let's Visit a Museum

Many people like to visit museums. They are great places to visit on the weekend. Some museums have interesting art. Some museums teach us about science.

The California Academy of Sciences in San Francisco, USA, is a science museum. It has places to learn about fossils, rocks, trees, and even dinosaurs! People can watch exciting movies about planets and stars at the planetarium.

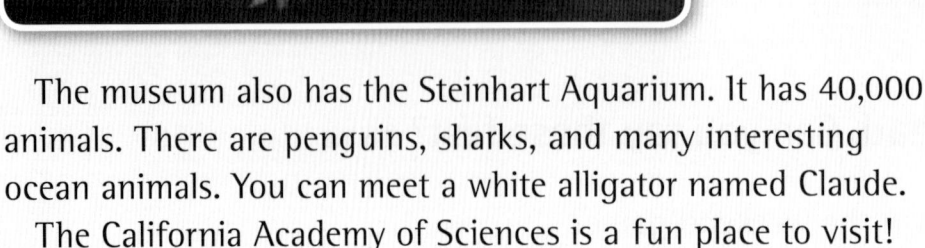

The museum also has the Steinhart Aquarium. It has 40,000 animals. There are penguins, sharks, and many interesting ocean animals. You can meet a white alligator named Claude.

The California Academy of Sciences is a fun place to visit!

2 Read. Check T for *True* or F for *False*.

1. The California Academy of Sciences is an art museum.   T   F
2. There are penguins at the aquarium.   T   F
3. The aquarium does not have many animals.   T   F
4. At the planetarium, you can watch movies about stars.   T   F

3 Read and write. What's at the California Academy of Sciences? Complete the graphic organizer.

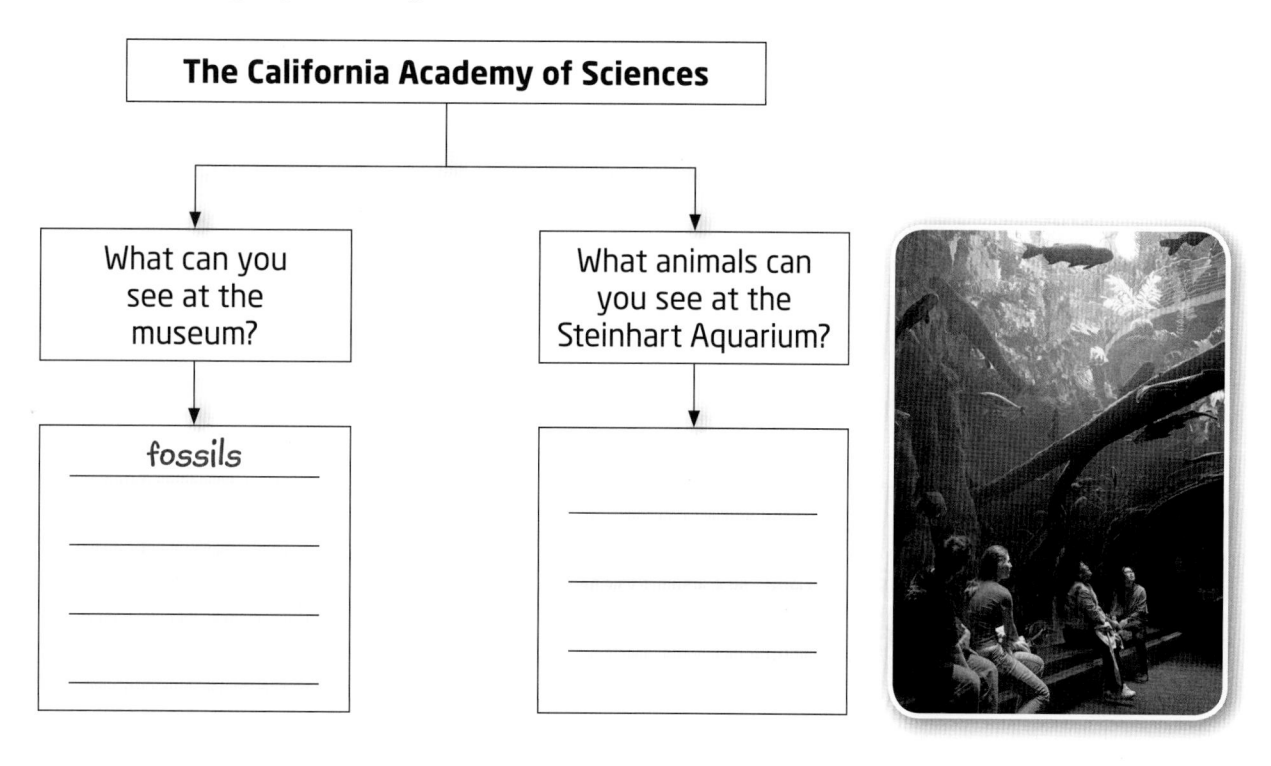

The California Academy of Sciences

What can you see at the museum?
- fossils
- _____
- _____
- _____

What animals can you see at the Steinhart Aquarium?
- _____
- _____
- _____

4 Complete the chart. Work with a partner. Ask and answer.

	Me	My partner
1. Do you want to visit a museum?		
2. What do you want to see there?		
3. Why are museums interesting places to visit?		

145

WRITING

1 **Read and write.** Read about Katya's busy afternoon. Underline the words that Katya uses to say when she did things.

My Busy Afternoon

Last Saturday afternoon was busy! First, I went on a picnic with my family. Next, I played in a soccer game. I was happy because my team won! After that, I went shopping with my mom. I bought new shoes. Then, I texted my friends, and we all went to a movie. After the movie, I went home. What a busy afternoon!

1. What did Katya do first?

   She _____.

2. What did Katya do next?

   She _____.

3. Did Katya text her friends before or after she went shopping?

   She _____.

2 **Write about a busy afternoon you had.** Tell when you did things. Use words like *first, then, next,* and *after.*

_____
_____
_____
_____
_____
_____
_____

146   Unit 9

UNIT 9 REVIEW

1 **Unscramble the sentences.** Write.

1. did / last / do / weekend? / you / What

   _____

2. stayed / home. / I

   _____

3. We / go / ice skating. / didn't

   _____

4. baseball, / She / team / played / win. / her / didn't / but

   _____

5. fishing / We / river. / the / in / went

   _____

6. museum? / visit / a / you / Did

   _____

2 **Look at the pictures.** Read and write.

1. Did the dog go horseback riding?

   The dog _____.

2. What did the dog do last weekend?

   The dog _____, _____,

   and _____.

3 **What about you?** What do you usually do on the weekend? Write.

I usually _____

_____.

Unit 6 Student 1: Use with Activity 3 on page 106.

3 Work with a partner. Complete the chart.

1. Look at the chart. Take turns asking and answering questions.
2. Write the questions and answers.

Is there any yogurt? — *Yes, there is a little.*

Questions	Answers
1. Is there any yogurt?	1. _Yes, there is a little._
2. _____	2. No, there aren't any.
3. Are there any bags of chips?	3. _____
4. _____	4. No, there isn't any.
5. Is there any orange juice?	5. _____
6. _____	6. Yes, there is a little.
7. Are there any bottles of oil?	7. _____

Look at the completed chart. What foods do you need to buy?

Unit 8 Student 1: Use with Activity 3 on page 130.

3 Work with a partner. Take turns asking and answering questions. Listen to your partner's answers. Write them.

Questions	Write your answers	Answer your partner's questions
1. Did Sara have a party?	1. _____	1. He went to Sara's party.
2. Did her friends come to the party?	2. _____	2. Yes, he rode his bike.
3. What did Sara's mom make?	3. _____	3. He wore a bathing suit.
4. Did Sara take photos?	4. _____	4. Yes, they swam at the party.
5. Did you see the photos?	5. _____	5. He gave her a birthday present.

Unit 5   Student 1: Use with Activity 3 on page 94.

3 **Work with a partner.** Take turns. Read your part of each sentence. Listen to your partner's part. Write it. Read the sentences together.

1. Crocodiles use their sharp teeth __to eat meat__.
2. _____ to shower.
3. Butterflies use their wings _____.
4. _____ to fight.
5. Crocodiles use their long, strong tails _____.

Unit 7   Student 1: Use with Activity 1 on page 119.

1 **Work with a partner.** Complete the paragraph.

1. Take turns reading sentences. Student 1 reads first.
2. Listen to your partner. Write the sentence.
3. Read the finished paragraph together.

I get enough exercise. _____ I don't eat too much junk food. _____ I drink enough water. _____ Do you?

Unit 9   Student 1: Use with Activity 2 on page 143.

2 **Work with a partner.** Take turns asking and answering. Listen to your partner's answers. Write the answers to complete the chart.

	Ken's Weekend	Leo's Weekend
1. What does Ken usually do on weekends?		Leo usually goes fishing.
2. What did Ken do last Saturday?		Leo didn't go fishing. He went hiking.
3. What did Ken do last Sunday?		Leo went swimming.

Unit 5 Student 2: Use with Activity 3 on page 94.

3 **Work with a partner.** Take turns. Read your part of each sentence. Listen to your partner's part. Write it. Read the sentences together.

1. _Crocodiles use their sharp teeth_ _____ to eat meat.
2. Elephants use their long trunks _____.
3. _____ to fly.
4. Sheep use their horns _____.
5. _____ to swim.

Unit 7 Student 2: Use with Activity 1 on page 119.

1 **Work with a partner.** Complete the paragraph.

1. Take turns reading sentences. Student 1 reads first.
2. Listen to your partner. Write the sentence.
3. Read the finished paragraph together.

_____ I don't watch too much TV. _____

_____ I eat enough vegetables. _____

I get enough rest. Do you?

Unit 9 Student 2: Use with Activity 2 on page 143.

2 **Work with a partner.** Take turns asking and answering. Listen to your partner's answers. Write the answers to complete the chart.

	Ken's Weekend	Leo's Weekend
1. What does Leo usually do on weekends?	Ken usually goes swimming.	
2. What did Leo do last Saturday?	Ken didn't go swimming. Ken went ice skating.	
3. What did Leo do last Sunday?	Ken went horseback riding.	

Unit 6   Student 2: Use with Activity 3 on page 106.

3 **Work with a partner.** Complete the chart.

1. Look at the chart. Take turns asking and answering questions.
2. Write the questions and answers.

> Is there any yogurt?

> Yes, there is a little.

Questions	Answers
1. _Is there any yogurt?_	1. Yes, there is a little.
2. Are there any jars of olives?	2. _____
3. _____	3. Yes, there are a few.
4. Is there any milk?	4. _____
5. _____	5. No, there isn't any.
6. Is there any meat?	6. _____
7. _____	7. No, there aren't any.

Look at the completed chart. What foods do you need to buy?

Unit 8   Student 2: Use with Activity 3 on page 130.

3 **Work with a partner.** Take turns asking and answering questions. Listen to your partner's answers. Write them.

Questions	Write your answers	Answer your partner's questions
1. Where did Hugo go?	1. _____	1. Yes, she had a party.
2. Did Hugo ride his bike to the party?	2. _____	2. Yes, they came to the party.
3. What did Hugo wear?	3. _____	3. She made a feast!
4. Did people swim at the party?	4. _____	4. No, her dad took photos.
5. What did Hugo give Sara?	5. _____	5. Yes, I saw them.

Unit 5 Cutouts Use with **GRAMMAR 2** Activity 2.

153

Unit 6 Cutouts Use with **GRAMMAR 2** Activity 2.

1   2   3

A

B

155

Unit 7 Cutouts Use with **GRAMMAR 2** Activity 2.

157

Unit 8 Cutouts Use with **GRAMMAR 2** Activity 2.

take	wear	took	wore
eat	drink	ate	drank
see	sing	saw	sang
go	have	went	had

Unit 9 Cutouts Use with **GRAMMAR 2** Activity 2.

161

My Words

Word	Picture
Word in my language	

Word	Picture
Word in my language	

Word	Picture
Word in my language	

Word	Picture
Word in my language	

Word	Picture
Word in my language	

Word	Picture
Word in my language	

My Words

Word	Picture
Word in my language	

Word	Picture
Word in my language	

Word	Picture
Word in my language	

Word	Picture
Word in my language	

Word	Picture
Word in my language	

Word	Picture
Word in my language	

My Words

Word	Picture
Word in my language	

Word	Picture
Word in my language	

Word	Picture
Word in my language	

Word	Picture
Word in my language	

Word	Picture
Word in my language	

Word	Picture
Word in my language	

My Words

Word	Picture
Word in my language	

Word	Picture
Word in my language	

Word	Picture
Word in my language	

Word	Picture
Word in my language	

Word	Picture
Word in my language	

Word	Picture
Word in my language	

My Words

Word	Picture
Word in my language	

Word	Picture
Word in my language	

Word	Picture
Word in my language	

Word	Picture
Word in my language	

Word	Picture
Word in my language	

Word	Picture
Word in my language	

My Words

Word	Picture
Word in my language	

Word	Picture
Word in my language	

Word	Picture
Word in my language	

Word	Picture
Word in my language	

Word	Picture
Word in my language	

Word	Picture
Word in my language	

Unit 5
stickers

Unit 6
stickers

Unit 7
stickers

Unit 8 stickers

Unit 9 stickers

CREDITS

Illustration

All illustrations © Cengage Learning

Photography

2 Nicolas Reusens/Moment/Getty Images; 4-5 (spread) © Ian Nichols; 6 (tl) Hugh Mackintosh/Gallo Images/Getty Images; (tc) Phil Schermeister/National Geographic Image Collection; (tr) David Noton Photography/Alamy Stock Photo; (cr) Matt Tilghman/Alamy Stock Photo; 6-7 (spread) John Warburton-Lee Photography/Alamy Stock Photo; 7 (tl) Ira Blcok/National Geographic Image Collection; (tc) Tommy Andersson/EyeEm/Getty Images; (tr) Denis-Huot/hemis.fr/Getty Images; (cl) Joel Sartore/National Geographic Image Collection; (cr) Ilene MacDonald/Alamy Stock Photo; (cl) Weimin Liu/Moment Select/Getty Images; (bl) Tom McHugh/Science Source; (bc) DigitalVision/Getty Images; (br) Charles Gullung/The Image Bank/Getty Images; 8-9 (spread) Quentin Martinez/Biosphoto/Getty Images; 10 (tl1) Tom Brakefield/Stockbyte/Getty Images; (tl2) Alaska Stock; (cl) Anup Shah/DigitalVision/Getty Images; (bl1) DigitalVision/Photodisc/Getty Images; (bl2) Manoj Shah/The Image Bank/Getty Images; 11 (bl) Andy119/Shutterstock.com; 12 (tl) LanStudios/Shutterstock.com; (tc1) Sergey Sklesnev/Alamy Stock Photo; (tr1) Kevin Giannini/Alamy Stock Photo; (tc2) Eastcott Momatiuk/Photodisc/Getty Images; (tr2) Andrew JK Tan/Moment/Getty Images; 14 (tl) Ian Shaw/Alamy Stock Photo; (cl) David Tipling/Minden Pictures; (bl1) Tom Brakefield/Stockbyte/Getty Images; (bl2) Gerald Nowak/The Image Bank/Getty Images; (br) Ralph Voltz/National Geographic Image Collection; 14-15 (spread) Rick Elkins/Moment/Getty Images; 16 (tr) Australian Scenics/Photolibrary/Getty Images; (cr1) Stu Porter/Alamy Stock Photo; (cr2) imageBroker/Alamy Stock Photo; 17 Anup Shah/Minden Pictures; 18 (tl) Mariano Ruiz/Dreamstime.com; (tr) Ravl/Dreamstime.com; 20-21 (spread) Stephane Ducandas; 22 (tr) Nico Tondini/Photographer's Choice/Getty Images; (cr) Laurence Mouton/PhotoAlto/Corbis; (br) VisitBritain/Ingrid Rasmussen/Getty Images; 22-23 (spread) fcafotodigital/E+/Getty Images; 23 (tl) Janko Bartolec/Dreamstime.com; (tr) Marin Bulat/Dreamstime.com; (cl) Paul Orr/Shutterstock.com; (cr) Rosemary Calvert/Photographer's Choice RF/Getty Images; (bl) Oleksiy Mark/Shutterstock.com; (br) Tina Wong/The Wandering Eater/Moment Open/Getty Images; 24-25 (spread) Jeff Greenberg/Universal Images Group/Getty Images; 26 mphillips007/E+/Getty Images; 27 fcafotodigital/E+/Getty Images; 28 (tl1) Findelmundo/Shutterstock.com; (tl2) Prachaya Roekdeethaweesab/Shutterstock.com; (tl3) Simon Mayer/Shutterstock.com; (tl4) Richard T. Nowitz/Corbis NX/Getty Images; (tc1) Steve Hix/Somos Images/Corbis; (tr1) Buena Vista Images/The Image Bank/Getty Images; (tc2) Chuck Pefley/Alamy Stock Photo; (tr2) Plattform/Johner Images/Corbis; 29 (bl1) iStock.com/jaminwell; (bl2) saurabhpbhoyar/Shutterstock.com; (bl3) Oleksiy Mark/Shutterstock.com; (bl4) iStock.com/kyoshino; (bl5) iStock.com/visual7; (bl6) iStock.com/Photokanok; (br1) iStock.com/Alexei Cruglicov/alexey_ds; (br2) iStock.com/nu-creation; (br3) iStock.com/Photokanok; (br4) D. Hurst/Alamy Stock Photo; (br5) iStock.com/jaminwell; (br6) iStock.com/visual7; 30 (tr1) (tr2) (cr) (br) © "What's for Lunch" - Andrea Curtis Photographs courtesy of Yvonne Duivenvoorden Inc.; 32 NYS/Shutterstock.com; 33 Ann and Steve Toon/NPL/Minden Pictures; 34 (tl1) Shkurd/Dreamstime.com; (tl2) Electrowan/Dreamstime.com; (bl) Christophe Testi/Dreamstime.com; (br1) Shkurd/Dreamstime.com; (br2) Christophe Testi/Dreamstime.com; 35 (c1) Christophe Testi/Dreamstime.com; (c2) Shkurd/Dreamstime.com; 36-37 (spread) Stephen Alvarez/National Geographic Image Collection; 38-39 (spread) Dozier Marc/hemis.fr/Getty Images; 40-41 (spread) Haziq Qadri/Barcroft Media/Getty Images; 42 (tl) uschools/E+/Getty Images; (tc) Todd Fong Photography/Moment Open/Getty Images; (tr) wong sze yuen/Shutterstock.com; (cl) Ryan McVay/DigitalVision/Getty Images; (c) Emena/Shutterstock.com; (cr) Anna Pekunova/Moment/Getty Images; 43 (bgd) John Fedele/Blend Images/Getty Images; 44 (tl) Alistair Berg/The Image Bank/Getty Images; (tc1) Elena Stepanova/Shutterstock.com; (tr1) Jose Luis Pelaez Inc/DigitalVision/Getty Images; (tc2) Jaren Jai Wicklund/Shutterstock.com; (tr2) Masterfile; 45 (tr) Vojta Herout/Shutterstock.com; (bl) Franco Vogt/Corbis/Getty Images; (bc) Susan Barr/Photolibrary/Getty Images; 46 (tr) Brian Mitchell/Corbis/Getty Images; (bgd) Tanja Voigt/Alamy Stock Photo; 47 (br) KathyDewar/E+/Getty Images; 48 Paul A. Souders/Corbis Documentary/Getty Images; 49 Olivier Renck/Aurora Photos; 50 (tl) Ravl/Dreamstime.com; (bl) Tatyana Vychegzhanina/Dreamstime.com; 51 (c) Zen Sekizawa/Taxi/Getty Images; (tc) RedChopsticks/redchopsticks/Getty Images; (bc) Jamie Grill/Photodisc/Getty Images; (br) Inti St Clair/Tetra images/Getty Images; 52-53 (spread) © Agota Kadar; 54 (tl) Susie Adams/Moment/Getty Images; (tc) Michael Kemp/Alamy Stock Photo; (cl) jeremy sutton-hibbert/Alamy Stock Photo; (c) Tonieo/Shutterstock.com; (bl) Edgardo Contreras/DigitalVision/Getty Images; 54-55 (spread) Ultra.F/The Image Bank/Getty Images; 55 (tl) Chabruken/The Image Bank/Getty Images; (tr) Jupiterimages/Stockbyte/Getty Images; (cl) Science Source/Getty Images; (c) Radius Images/Getty Images; (bl) Kate Mitchell/Spirit/Corbis; (br) Judy Bellah/Alamy Stock Photo; 56-57 (spread) Jan Sochor/LatinContent Editorial/Getty Images; 58 Im ChanKyung/Topic Images/Getty Images; 60 (tl) iStock.com/egal; (tc1) C Squared Studios/Stockbyte/Getty Images; (tr1) Elena Schweitzer/Shutterstock.com; (tc2) iStock.com/trigga; (tr2) Mike Flippo/Shutterstock.com; 62 (bgd) ElCorazon Photo/Shutterstock.com; (tr) Christian Kober/robertharding/Getty Images; (cr) Daniel Osterkamp/Moment/Getty Images; 64 Masaaki Tanka/amana images/Getty Images; 65 Toni Anzenberger/Redux; 66 (tl) Peter Langer/Perspectives/Getty Images; (tr1) Peter Langer/Perspectives/Getty Images; (tr2) Olivier Chouchana/Gamma-Rapho/Getty Images; (tr3) Peter Langer/Perspectives/Getty Images; (tr4) Peter Langer/Perspectives/Getty Images; (bl1) Garsya/Dreamstime.com; (bl2) iStock.com/JoKMedia; (bl3) Feng Yu/Dreamstime.com; (bl4) Ravl/Dreamstime.com; (bl5) Tatyana Vychegzhanina/Dreamstime.com; (br1) Tatyana Vychegzhanina/Dreamstime.com; (br2) Ravl/Dreamstime.com; (br3) Feng Yu/Dreamstime.com; (br4) iStock.com/JoKMedia; 68-69 (spread) © Shivesh Ram; 70 (tl) TongRo Images/Alamy Stock Photo; (cl) Ale Ventura/PhotoAlto/AGE Fotostock; (cr) Amy Toensing/National Geographic Image Collection; (bl) Andersen Ross Photography Inc/DigitalVision/Getty Images; (br) White Packert/Photographer's Choice/Getty Images; 70-71 (spread) Reed Kaestner/Corbis/Getty Images; 71 (tr) Barry Austin/Photodisc/Getty Images; (tr) Lori Adamski Peek/The Image Bank/Getty Images; (cl) Tom & Dee Ann McCarthy/Corbis/Getty Images; (cr) Anthony Bradshaw/Photodisc/Getty Images; (bl) Tim Klein/Stockbyte/Getty Images; (br) uniquely india/photosindia/Getty Images; 72-73 (spread) Timothy Allen/Photonica World/Getty Images; 74 Hero Images/Getty Images; 76 (tl) Stock Connection Blue/Alamy Stock Photo; (tc1) Peter Cade/The Image Bank/Getty Images; (tr1) Anne Ackermann/The Image Bank/Getty Images; (tc2) imagewerks/Imagewerks Japan/Getty Images; (tr2) Mike Brinson/The Image Bank/Getty Images; 77 (br) money & coins/ian sanders/Alamy Stock Photo; 78 (cr) Children's Museum of Indianapolis; (bgd) David R. Frazier Photolibrary, Inc./Alamy Stock Photo; 80 (tr) Paul Brown/Alamy Stock Photo; (cr) AFP Contributor/Getty Images; 81 Chung Sung-Jun/Getty Images News/Getty Images; 82 (tr1) Tatyana Vychegzhanina/Dreamstime.com; (tr2) Feng Yu/Dreamstime.com; (tr3) Ravl/Dreamstime.com; (bl1) Tatyana Vychegzhanina/Dreamstime.com; (bl2) Feng Yu/Dreamstime.com; (bl3) Ravl/Dreamstime.com; (bl4) Christophe Testi/Dreamstime.com; 83 (tc1) Jenny Elia Pfeiffer/Corbis; (tc2) Image Source/Corbis; 84-85 (spread) BrAt82/Shutterstock.com; 85 (tl1) Jack.Q/Shutterstock.com; (tl2) Matt Knoth/Shutterstock.com; (cl1) Kathryn Simons/Shutterstock.com; (cl2) Scott Buckel/Alamy Stock Photo; 86-87 (spread) Ian MacNicol/Getty Images Sport/Getty Images; 88 (tl) Ilene MacDonald/Alamy Stock Photo; (tc) Weimin Liu/Moment Select/Getty Images; (tr) Charles Gullung/The Image Bank/Getty Images; (bl) Tommy Andersson/EyeEm/Getty Images; (bc) Ira Block/National Geographic Image Collection; (br) Hugh Mackintosh/Gallo Images/Getty Images; 89 (tl) Matt Tilghman/Alamy Stock Photo; (tc) Joel Sartore/National Geographic Image Collection; (tr) John Warburton-Lee Photography/Alamy Stock Photo; (cl) Tom McHugh/Science Source; (c) Phil Schermeister/National Geographic Image Collection; (cr) David Noton Photography/Alamy Stock Photo; (bc1) Denis-Huot/hemis.fr/Getty Images; (bc2) DigitalVision/Getty Images; 90 (tl) Pyty/Shutterstock.com; (tc) Steve Williams Photo/Stone/Getty Images; (tr) Alaska Stock/; 91 (tr1) iStock.com/Cinoby; (tr2) Manoj Shah/The Image Bank/Getty Images; (cr1) Berndt Fischer/Oxford Scientific/Getty Images; (cr2) iStock.com/Cinoby; (br1) imageBroker/Alamy Stock Photo; (bc) Lopolo/Shutterstock.com; (br2) Safique Hazarika Photography/Moment Open/Getty Images; (br3) iStock.com/Sandsun; 92 (tl) Pat Bennett/Alamy Stock Photo; (tc) Maximilian Weinzierl/Alamy Stock Photo; (tl) Paul & Paveena Mckenzie/Oxford Scientific/Getty Images; (cr1) Martin Harvey/Photodisc/Getty Images; (c2) FLPA/Alamy Stock Photo; 93 (cl) Ernie Janes/Alamy Stock Photo; (c) Ocean/Corbis; (cr) SuperStock/Alamy Stock Photo; (bc1) Gerry Ellis/Media bakery; (bc2) GK Hart/Vikki Hart/Corbis; 96 (tr) Stefan Christmann/Corbis NX/Getty Images; (cr) Hannes G/Shutterstock.com; (br) iStock.com/Mediarich; 97 Alaska Stock; 100 (tr) iStock.com/Julichka; (bc1) iStock.com/Dlerick; 101 (tl) iStock.com/Hilmi_m; (tc) iStock.com/Nicolebranan; (tr) Janko Bartolec/Dreamstime.com; (cl) iStock.com/esolla; (c) iStock.com/Luismmolina; (cr) iStock.com/scanrail; (bl) iStock.com/HelpingHandPhotos; (bc2) karel_/iStock/Getty Images; 107 (cl) Richard T. Nowitz/Corbis NX/Getty Images; (cr) Fuse/Corbis/Getty Images; (bl) Plattform/Johner Images Royalty-Free/Getty Images; (bc) Chuck Pefley/Alamy Siock Photo; (br) Ken Gillespie Photography/Alamy Stock Photo; 108 (tl) XiXinXing/Shutterstock.com; (br) Anna_Pustynnikova/Shutterstock.com; 109 dpa picture alliance archive/Alamy Stock Photo; 110 iStock.com/DebbiSmirnoff; 111 (tl) Nico Tondini/Photographer's Choice/Getty Images; (tc) Janko Bartolec/Dreamstime.com; (tr) Marin Bulat/Dreamstime.com; 112-113 (spread) Mike Kemp/Alamy Stock Photo; 114 (tl) Serega K Photo and Video/Shutterstock.com; (tc) Design Pics/SW Productions/Getty Images; (tr) Klaus Tiedge/Blend Images/Getty Images; 117 (cl) ImagesBazaar/Getty Images; (cr) Eco Images/Universal Images Group/Getty Images; (bl) Ljupco Smokovski/Shutterstock.com; (br) FamVeld/Shutterstock.com; 118 (tr) iStock.com/RyanKing999; (cr) Blend Images - Kris Timken/Tetra images/Getty Images; (bl) Oleksiy Mark/Shutterstock.com; (br) RayArt Graphics/Alamy Stock Photo; 120 NHPA/Science Source; 122 Ewa Studio/Shutterstock.com; 124 (cl) Ultra.F/The Image Bank/Getty Images; (c) iStock.com/Biscut; (cr) Eddie Gerald/Alamy Stock Photo; (bl) Lopolo/Shutterstock.com; (bc) Susie Adams/Moment/Getty Images; (br) Radius Images/Getty Images; 125 (tl) Chabruken/The Image Bank/Getty Images; (tr) Ira Block/National Geographic/Getty Images; (bc) Liu Liqun/Corbis Documentary/Getty Images; (cl) Kate Mitchell/Spirit/Corbis; (c) Blend Images - JGI/Jamie Grill/Tetra images/Getty Images; (cr) Andrea Pistolesi/The Image Bank/Getty Images; 126 (tr) Judy Bellah/Alamy Stock Photo; (cr1) waldru/iStock/Getty Images; (cr2) jeremy sutton-hibbert/Alamy Stock Photo; 127 Richard Lewisohn/Photodisc/Getty Images; 128 Best View Stock/Getty Images; 129 Imagemore Co., Ltd./Imagemore/Getty Images; 132 (tc) Malin Holm/Maskot/Getty Images; (tr) Chad Ehlers/Alamy Stock Photo; (cr) Joensson Alf/WoodyStock/Alamy Stock Photo; 134 Richard Levine/Alamy Stock Photo; 136 (tl) Iakov Filimonov/Shutterstock.com; (tr) wavebreakmedia ltd/Shutterstock.com; (bl) Deborah Faulkner/Moment/Getty Images; (br) Seth Joel/Photographer's Choice RF/Getty Images; 137 (tl) Fancy/Veer/Corbis/Getty Images; (tr) PhotoAlto/Ale Ventura/Getty Images; (cl) Paul Barton/Getty Images; 138 (tr1) Andersen Ross/Photodisc/Getty Images; (tr2) Elisabeth Schmitt/Flickr Open/Getty Images; (cl) imagewerks/Imagewerks Japan/Getty Images; (c) ER Productions Limited/DigitalVision/Getty Images; (cr1) Peter Cade/The Image Bank/Getty Images; (cr2) Stock Connection Blue/Alamy Stock Photo; 140 (cr1) iStock.com/joel-t; (c1) uniquely india/photosindia/Getty Images; (cr2) Andersen Ross Photography Inc/DigitalVision/Getty Images; (c2) White Packert/Photographer's Choice/Getty Images; (br1) Tim Klein/Stockbyte/Getty Images; (br2) Barry Austin/Photodisc/Getty Images; 141 (tl) Monkey Business Images/Shutterstock.com; (tc) Iliana Mestari/Moment/Getty Images; (tr) rtbilder/Shutterstock.com; (cl) Mike Brinson/The Image Bank/Getty Images; (c) Chris Stein/DigitalVision/Getty Images; 144 (tl) Gary Crabbe/Alamy Stock Photo; (bl) Alice Musbach/Alamy Stock Photo; 145 Kris Davidson/Lonely Planet Images/Getty Images; 153 (tl) iStock.com/Dirk Freder; (tc) Andrew JK Tan/Moment/Getty Images; (tr) iStock.com/tomodaji; (cl1) Eastcott Momatiuk/Photodisc/Getty Images; (c1) Sharon Montrose/Photodisc/Getty Images; (cl2) iStock.com/skilpad; (c2) iStock.com/namibelephant; (cl3) iStock.com/vblinov; (c3) iStock.com/Sarah_Cheriton; (bl) iStock.com/Blend_Images; (bc) iStock.com/skynesher; (br) Stanod/Dreamstime.com; 155 (tl) iStock.com/MargoeEdwards; (cl1) saurabhpbhoyar/Shutterstock.com; (c1) D. Hurst/Alamy Stock Photo; (tr1) iStock.com/visual7; (cr1) iStock.com/kyoshino; (cr2) Oleksiy Mark/Shutterstock.com; 21 iStock.com/Alexei Cruglicov/alexey_ds; (bl) iStock.com/nu-creation; (bc) iStock.com/Photokanok; (br) iStock.com/jaminwell; 157 (tl) Onoky - Photononstop/Alamy Stock Photo; (tc) Corbis/VCG/Getty Images; (tr) Susan Barr/Photolibrary/Getty Images; (cl1) Brian Hagiwara/Photolibrary/Getty Images; (a1) allstars/Shutterstock.com; (c1) Aprilphoto/Shutterstock.com; (c2) Ty Allison/Photographer's Choice/Getty Images; (cr2) Franco Vogt/Corbis/Getty Images; (cr2) Spencer Jones/Photographer's Choice/Getty Images; (bl) Fuse/Corbis/Getty Images; (bc) (br) Masterfile; 161 (tc) Kevin Dodge/Corbis/Getty Images; (cl) ERproductions Ltd/Blend Images/Corbis; (tr) Tamara Lackey/fstop/Corbis; (cl1) Jose Luis Pelaez Inc/DigitalVision/Getty Images; (c1) Gardel Bertrand/hemis.fr/Getty Images; (cr1) RPM Pictures/The Image Bank/Getty Images; (cl2) Ascent/PKS Media Inc./Getty Images; (c2) Ascent/PKS Media Inc./Getty Images; (cr2) Donald Iain Smith/Moment/Getty Images; (bl) Radius Images/Corbis; (bc) Patrik Giardino/Corbis/Getty Images; (br) PhotoAlto/Eric Audras/Getty Images.